J.W Mahony

England's Falling Workshop, etc.

Industrial Chart and Proposed Act of Parliament

J.W Mahony

England's Falling Workshop, etc.
Industrial Chart and Proposed Act of Parliament

ISBN/EAN: 9783337155629

Printed in Europe, USA, Canada, Australia, Japan

Cover: Foto ©ninafisch / pixelio.de

More available books at **www.hansebooks.com**

ENGLAND'S FALLING WORKSHOP,

ETC.

Industrial Chart, and Proposed Act of Parliament.

BY

J. W. MAHONY.

LONDON:
HARRING PUBLISHING COMPANY,
82, Southampton Row, W. C.

1893.

It is safe to postulate that no question, concerning which a difference of opinion exists, has been so misunderstood, or so strongly misrepresented, as the subject of England's policy of Free-Imports—commonly, but inaccurately, defined as Free-Trade. The principle of free-trade, *i.e.*, free-exchange, has been in the past almost hopelessly confused with the British fiscal system of partial free-imports. The working classes of Great Britain have been taught to believe that a policy of free ports for all competing imports, is the cause of all the industrial prosperity and social progress of the last half century. This statement and other vain-glorious assertions are notoriously untrue; but the false belief has been so firmly implanted in the minds of the masses during the last forty years, by means of millions of misleading leaflets and newspaper propaganda, that it will need a strong and a vigorous effort on the part of the true economic educators to eradicate the deep-rooted errors and misconceptions which have stood in the path of fiscal reform.

To state the present position of Great Britain's industrial and commercial interests in the mildest terms, one has to admit the grave fiscal isolation in which those interests are placed. Economically unarmed amid keen industrial rivals triply armoured with hostile tariffs, free ports, and reciprocity treaties, England stands defenceless. Will the blind and foolish cant of free-trade defend us in the coming hour of trial? The world at large understands perfectly well what free-trade is, and they know it to be as unattainable as universal peace, and as measurably purchasable as modern peace periods, and on the same principle of ever-readiness for war.

Great Britain has the power to compel a large measure of approximate free-trade by declaring a tariff-war upon her industrial rivals, and by a commercial union of her Colonies and Possessions.

The power of those British Capitalists who have investments abroad, must be broken, and Britain's economic and fiscal freedom will speedily follow.

The present writer has had ample opportunities during the last four years, to guage the knowledge and the teachableness of the working classes on the subject, and it is certain, beyond all controversy, that a great change is coming upon the British people concerning our bastard system of free-trade.

The full and well-paid employment of the masses of the people is the pressing and the burning political problem of the time. Free-imports, as a permanent policy, is doomed. Trade-Unionists are advancing upon it in a " backstairs " way, by their trades-union—rate-of-wages clause in public contracts. But the British Electorate will finally seal its doom at the Parliamentary Ballot-Box.

J. W. MAHONY.

BIRMINGHAM, 1893.

	PAGE
England's Workshop falling like a House of Cards	7
Labour Interests and Free-Imports	30
To Enforce, not forsake, Free-Trade	43
Why I oppose the policy of Free-Imports	63
Free Trade without Freedom	72
(An open Letter to Lord Salisbury).	
Free-Trade a living sham	75
(An open Letter to Mr. W. E. Gladstone).	
Our Free-Importing System	77
(An open Letter to Mr. Joseph Chamberlain).	
United Empire and Better Trade	80
(A Reply to the Cobden Club Leaflet, No. 88).	
The Agricultural Crisis	88
(A Word to Agriculturalists and the Public).	
An Open Letter to Trade-Uuionists	91
Sham Free-Trade	94
(An Address to Working Men).	
British Free-Trade	99
(A Dialogue between two Working Men).	
The Chief Opponents of Shorter Hours of Labour	104
(An open Letter to the British Advocates of an Eight-hours Day)	
When is Food Cheap?	112
Reform, or Industrial Revolution. Which?	123
Proposed Act of Parliament to enforce Free-Trade	139

ERRATA :—*Omit hyphen in free labour, on page 42.*
Insert, not, after did—fifth line, page 128.

As Free Trade does not exist, can the policy of Free Imports be defended ?

BRITAIN'S STARVING WORKERS SUPPLY THE ANSWER!

"ENGLAND'S WORKSHOP FALLING LIKE A HOUSE OF CARDS."

A Speech delivered in the Lesser Free-Trade Hall, Manchester, February 29th, 1893.

It is, I venture to think, an advantage of no inconsiderable importance, that I make my first appearance before a Manchester audience as the representative of no political section or party, but simply as the advocate of a great question affecting the welfare of all sections of the industrial community, and one that must be dealt with by the nation in the immediate future. I know not the particular mode in which the question may be brought into practical politics, but I am free to state that, I will follow any political party in the country that will move as such, and place the cause in the forefront of their programme and write it upon their banners. I say this much, because I regard the question of the industrial interests of the United Kingdom as overshadowingly greater than any existing or imaginary political policy. Coming to the question before us, the one of England's Falling Workshop.

It has been, and still is, the custom to describe the condition of British trade as being depressed or as passing through an acute phase of depression This is an inadequate description, and comes of a general want of national and world-wide knowledge of the economic conditions of the labour and industrial centres of the earth. The words used on such occasions should convey a truthful impression of the actual circumstances of the situation, so that the eyes of the people may be opened to the gravity of the danger which threatens them. British trade is not simply in a depressed state, it is in a condition of collapse.

This statement and the gravity of the case can be sustained by an array of facts, and by various branches of evidence of an overwhelming character. It may be thought that this description of Britain's labour market is too pessimistic, even for a city, which has, it is said, run the vein of pessemism dry. But the facts I shall adduce, will show it to be true and not over-drawn Give your attention for a moment to the sad plight to which all our staple industries are reduced No not one of the whole list but what suffers from a chronic stagnation Apart from the special local circumstances which accentuate the dreadful state of your great cotton industry at the present time, take the condition of the iron and the steel trades, cutlery, pottery, woollen, silk, hardware, and ship-building industries, and what do you find ? Why an equal state of collapse, second to that of the national and basic industry of agriculture itself. Since all the staple trades are suffering alike, is it too much to say that the workshop of England is falling to pieces? I know that there are persons who assert that if the workers would take less wages trade would revive. The truth which lies in this statement opens up a serious question, a question which is best stated when I say that the subject of reduction in wages is one of civilization and barbarism.

I admit that if British workmen would consent to work at a sufficiently low rate of wages that plenty of work could be commanded. But what is the true meaning of the constant lowering of wages? Unless the production of a great nation trading like England is based on an economically sound foundation as regards internal taxation and freedom from hostile tarifls, a five per cent. reduction to-day, points to another five per cent. to-morrow, and a still further sacrifice a little later on until the lowest labour level of the world was reached. I, therefore, support men who strike against a reduction of wages when there is no sign of a speedy return to old rates, because it is the only means to resist barbarism. I sympathise with the men in their manful endeavour to preserve the measure of civilization which they at present enjoy, and not be driven back in the scale of social life. Better to die in resisting social and industrial slavery, than succumb and live in misery under it. In saying this do not suppose that I am indifferent to the trials and the trouble that have fell to the share of the manufacturers and their families. Their lot is hard also. But we must look to the real underlying causes which are producing all the industrial evils, and trace the promoters of them. The thirteen millions of workers who constitute, with their families, the mass of the nation, who in fact make the nation, must have their interest considered before that of a comparatively small section of capitalists, who are exploiting the lower labour levels of the backward races of the world, using our brains or our inventions, to enter into competition with the socially-advanced British worker to his degradation and ruin. A thorough examination is needed of the system of international trading which has governed our commercial intercourse with the world, and also a clear insight into the economic conditions of modern production in the chief industrial nations. It is not the British manufacturer and the English artizan who have the control of the conditions which govern international exchange, but the foreign tariff makers and the British foreign investors.

In order to guage the position of England's workshop to-day, as compared with the period when the title of "workshop of the world" was a living reality, I will take the first two years of the four phenomenally prosperous ones, viz., 1871-2-3-4, and contrast them, as regards our exports of British and Irish products, with the two years just ended, 1891-2. In the years 1871-2 we increased our exports by the enormous sum of fifty-seven millions stirling. From 199 millions in 1870, to 256 millions in 1872. During the last two years the exports of British and Irish products have decreased thirty-six millions sterling. From 263 millions in 1890, to 227 millions in 1892. The full meaning of this statement of facts will be seen in its true light as it affects British workers when I tell you that with a population of seven millions greater in 1892 than in 1872, the exports from Britain's workshop have fallen off to the enormous extent of twenty-nine millions sterling as compared with twenty years ago.*

This heavy shrinkage in our exports of British goods during the years named would not have seriously affected the English producer if our own markets had increased in a corresponding degree. But in this respect we have received an even greater check to the productions of the British fields and workshops, for during the past score years the imports of fully-manufactured articles which compete with us has more than doubled, while the striking increase in the competing food imports has added a still further curtailment of the demand for the products of British labour. The greater part of these foreign supplies of food has displaced agricultural labour without affording adequate compensation by creating an equal

---

* Of course some allowance must be made for the fall in prices since 1872. But it should be remembered that a great shrinkage in value often imperils an industry by turning a profit into a loss.

demand for the goods of the British artizan. Food imported does not benefit the worker in the town to anything like the extent as in the case of home-raised food, because the foreign supply comes here in great part, as the payment of interest on British capital invested abroad, and does not, therefore, require English goods in payment.

It must from these facts be quite clear to you that the demand for goods from the British workshop is not simply declining a little, but is in several quarters ceasing altogether. What then is the future prospect for the British worker, the proud citizen of a country which has stood in the vanguard of civilization and given to the world representative institutions and many of the enduring arts of peace ? Has he any reasonable hope that English trade will revive without any effort on his part, and that industrial affairs will right themselves ? From which quarter of the globe does he expect a demand for British goods ? Is it from France or Germany, Austria, Belgium, Russia, Italy, or the United States of America ? No one can be any longer in ignorance of the fact that these industrial rivals of Great Britain are not only determined to manufacture all that they may require for their own use, but they also intend to supply each other reciprocally, and also to compete with England in neutral markets. They have made treaties with each other, and with the Governments of undeveloped countries for the monopoly of their trade to the exclusion of the goods of the United Kingdom.* The United States of America is the most enterprising in this respect, and has contracted commercial agreements with many nations, including Germany, and the time is near at hand when they will, unless we forestall them, obtain a commercial treaty with Canada, which would mean a differential tariff against the mother country. After such an event, as that, our Australian Colonies after federating with themselves would follow the example of the Canadian dominion and do the best for their country's interest. It is the economic law of our time.

Where are our future markets? Bad as our trade is, can we even retain what we have left? I have glanced over the great nations of the earth, and have, I think, shown you that our case must become worse and worse under existing conditions We of all people fold our arms and wait for commercial affairs to settle themselves. We are in the position of a man playing at cards with a number of others who are allowed to make their own rules, and even to cheat should they feel so disposed. To win at such a game is hopeless. To lose is certain

It would be well at this point to consider the conditions under which England built up

---

* Note the commercial treaties entered into between the United States of America and Brazil and Cuba since the passing of the McKinley Act, by virtue of which a preference of twenty-five per cent. in import duties is conceded to many of the exports of the former, as compared with the tariff levied on goods from Great Britain.

her great export trade in the past. There were, roughly speaking, three leading advantages which this country possessed over the rest of the world. First, our start in mechanical inventions and labour-saving appliances. Secondly, our vast and precious mineral resources, and, Thirdly, our enormous wealth in gold and bullion These circumstances made us practical dictators of the world's method of exchange. We were enabled to exchange the products of one day's labour with that of three days work of the foreigner. This advantage, the foreign trader resolved to wrest from us at the earliest opportunity. And this desire was quite rational. The workshop of the world might reasonably have expected a modification of its dimensions, but not a sudden collapse. Yet we have lived to see it, and to witness the departure of all the advantages we once enjoyed singly Our inventions have been universally diffused. Our minerals are no longer kept as a monopoly, and our gold is distributed over the entire surface of the earth.

We do not complain of the world's development, but of the signal and gross injustice to which the products of the British worker are subjected in the home and the foreign markets of the globe. It has, at length, become a question of life and death, and self-preservation calls for strong measures.

This country conducts her external trade on the policy called Free-Trade. The policy of throwing open our markets was advocated as a means of removing restrictions to the commercial intercourse of nations, with the enlightened view of developing the resources of the earth and of hastening the day of peace and good-will among men. With that view of the matter I am in hearty agreement. I am a free-trader, and trust that you are all free-traders in that sense. I am here in this hall, which has been dedicated to the principle of free-trade, to uphold free-trade and to further its application. But I deny that free-trade exists in this country. A policy of free-imports to Dutch-auction the surplus goods of the globe, while the labour products of the British worker are ruinously taxed in every port in the world, is not free-trade Free-trade, is free-selling as well as free-buying. Of what use is it to buy your food and your raw material in an untaxed market, if your manufactured articles are crushed to death on the other side by hostile tariffs? Where are the free markets for British goods? Every one must be acquainted with the fact that no free-markets exist for English exports. There is no free-trade. As free-trade does not exist, can the policy of free-imports be defended? Let no man call himself a free-trader who defends free-imports without free-exports. Free-imports as an isolated policy cannot be defended. It is condemned by our million-and-a-half of starving workers, and the world's restrictive measures and protective practices. Free-trade should sweep away restrictions. Real free-trade would do so. A policy of free-imports has caused barriers to be raised against British exports which did not formerly exist. British trade, both internal and external, is fettered and hindered so far as English productions are concerned to a greater extent than has ever been known, and yet some persons foolishly think that we have free-trade. The melancholy fact must be stated that those who should lead and teach, our Members of Parliament, are themselves either ignorant or afraid of the subject. You must, therefore, perfect your own knowledge of the question, and then endeavour to instruct your Representatives. We are sometimes told by persons who constitute themselves authorities on this matter, that if we cannot obtain free-trade on both sides, that it is better to have it on our side than not have any free-trade at all. This sounds plausible enough. But let us look into it closely. To take their position at its best, I will refer to an illustration that has been used in this connection. A bridge spanning a river to unite two towns, having a toll-house at each end of the bridge, is given as a representation of two nations taxing each other by tariffs. It is better, so it is argued, to have one toll abolished than to maintain the two. If this illustration were an exact parallel to the case of nations with tariffs, it might appear to work out favourably for the contention. But to take the illustration of the double toll on a bridge as giving some small example of the working of free-imports and the actual effects of the policy on the fixed action of the nations trading with

Great Britain, we must suppose that the town at the end of the bridge, which retains the toll, no sooner discovers the abolition of the toll at the opposite end of the bridge and the advantage of entering the other town free to sell their wares, than they decide to treble their toll and make the people from the town at the free end of the bridge pay 50 per cent. more to trade with their neighbour than they did when the double toll existed. And to render the example entirely accurate you have further to suppose that the toll town permitted its own citizens to pass along the bridge without paying toll, exacting this, only from the free-town people. In this working of the example you have a very fair illustration of the influence and effects of the British policy of free-imports.

This international system of trading which is carried on by the bastard free-traders, has heights and depths, which at first sight do not appear. The reform of the policy is a life and death question. It means nothing less than the life and civilization of the people of Great Britan.

I have spoken of the exploiting of the lower labour levels of the people of the world, which our system of free-imports encouraged. I will now refer to a branch of British industry, which is threatened with extinction by the low wages of a backward and subject race. It is known to some of you that in the period immediately following upon the quelling of the Indian Mutiny a start was made by some British capitalists to spin and weave cotton cloth in and around the district of Bombay. An import duty on cotton goods, for revenue, which was maintained until 1875, greatly favoured this venture. The growth of the Indian cotton industry, in which native workers are employed at 7d. and 8d. per day, from sun-rise to sun-set, will be apparent when I state that in 1885 there were 87 mills, 16,000 power looms, upwards of two millions of spindles, 67,000 operatives, and an annual consumption of raw cotton of two millions cwts. This scale of progress sinks into insignificance, beside the rate of increase in the five following years, from 1885 to 1890, the last year for which I possess statistics. During these five years the 87 mills increased to 137, while the power looms augmented from 16,000 to 23,000, the spindles from 2,000,000 to 3,500,000, the number of operatives rose from 67,000 to 102,000 and the consumption of raw cotton went up from two millions to 3,500,000 cwts. To guage the relative progress of this Indian cotton industry, we have but to compare the consumption of raw cotton of this Eastern competition with that of Great Britain. The consumption of raw cotton in India in 1890 was nearly one-third of the total of our importation of that material from the United States These facts will justify my charge in relation to the exploitation of lower labour levels. It makes little difference that this Indian manufacture of cotton goods is for the native markets. They are competitors just the same as if the products of their spindles came here. Any rival in the supply of goods to markets which we have made our own has to be taken into account as affecting our labour interests. The rate of wages paid, and the general condition under which each of our rivals produce their goods are matters of immediate concern to us If India, with its cheap native labour, has made such enormous progress as to displace nearly two millions sterling of British cotton goods in one year, what of the future? To reduce our export of cotton goods to India from 18 millions sterling to 16 millions, as was the case in 1891, is a very serious matter. Can we assign any probable limit to the growth of cotton cloth manufacture in India? I say that we cannot fix such limit. Unless the conditions are altered, Indian manufacturers will not only supply India, China, and Japan with cotton goods, but I prophesy that before the 20th century is a few years old, Indian cotton cloth will displace the produce of British cotton operatives in the English market itself. It is merely a question of the further extension of the industry in our dependency, and Great Britain in this particular will be swamped. What other markets would the Indian manufacturers be able to supply? Would they be able to send their cheap cotton goods to France and Germany, or the United States of America? No they would not, because those nations would raise walls of tariffs, higher and higher, and still higher, to shut out the " tendencies of barbarism." They would not permit their people to be robbed of their labour by the products of such Eastern slavery. In saying this I do not wish to disparage the poor Hindoo. I pity him and would help to raise him in the social and industrial scale. If, however, we must compete with the cheap labour of India, we at least have the right to insist that the same factory legislation which governs the textile industry in the United Kingdom, shall be enforced in the case of the Indian operatives. And I would urge that in this matter of employing the subject races of India, we would do well to find them labour in an occupation for which, by nature and position, they are most fitted. They should be employed in growing the raw cotton for our market. This should, in my opinion, be encouraged by an English bounty to all Indian cotton reaching ports to be used in British manufacture. This would be better statesmanship than to permit the present ruinous competition between Indian and British labour. Which, I may ask, is the more important? The profit of the British capitalist in the cotton manufacture in India, or the work and the civilization of hundreds of thousands of cotton operatives in England? The danger of our policy of free imports is of an ever-increasing character. In the future of the Indian cotton industry we are, by our open ports, threatened with the ruin of our foreign and home trade in cotton cloth, and the displaced operatives will have no alternative industries to resort to, because the same policy of bastard free-trade has destroyed each and all of the country's staple trades In the fanatical adherence to a system of international trading, which appeared to succeed in the past, on account of the wars and the backwardness of our present commercial rivals, lies the danger to the workers of Great Britain.

It is not generally known that the existing policy of free imports of all competing goods is but nineteen years old. The year 1875 was the first year in which free ports were thrown open to the surplus goods of the world. The question has never been fought out. The people of Great Britain have never sanctioned free-imports as a permanent policy. The only formal assent given by the nation was to the anti-corn law. The inauguration of free-trade on our side has had but a passive toleration, and with the expectation that our example would be followed by other nations. The people of these Islands still desire free-trade, not the outrageous travesty of it, such as we have at present, but a real unfettered and unrestricted system of commercial exchange which would benefit the nation's industries in all their branches. Unfettered free exchange which most of you will believe in, and deem most desirable, is not favoured by a few specially wise ones, who, while upholding the principle of free-trade in some respects, are constantly asserting that it would be a bad thing for the country if the United States of America adopted the system and let in the exports of England and other nations free of duty. This is a strange aspect of the case. Here are men, calling themselves free-traders, who cry out against free-trade. The United States have not to adopt free-trade, as they possess it already in its complete form, and it is this great fact which underlies the extraordinary rate of industrial progress which has marked the development of that country during the past thirty years. The American people have unlimited free-trade in their forty-nine States and Territories and among their own population of 65 millions, and they are seeking to extend it all over the American Continent by treaties, etc. It is true, that it is conditioned free-trade. Internally free, and externally defended. Their system of free-trade is protected from the inroad of the products of what they term the pauper labour of England and Europe.

The American citizens, however, much as they may differ among themselves about the amount of tariffs, are united in keeping out the cheaper class of goods made by the low-paid labour of England and other countries. And yet, in despite of this united wisdom of the Americans, who at least should know their own business, a few wise ones in this country—Stock brokers and others—say that the tariffs set up at the American ports are a good thing for the British producer, as they prevent the workers in the United States from beating us out of the neutral markets of the world. They would, however, have us believe on our side, that it is a benefit to us to be shut out of the American markets, and they endeavour to persuade the

Americans that their tariffs are the only barriers to the indefinite increase of their manufactures for the whole world.

Such is the reasoning of some of the supporters of the English policy of free-imports. We may easily upset this foolish vein of thought. We possess the very system which they assert would enable the Americans to capture the markets of all nations. Are we able to command an increasing export trade? A falling off of 36 millions sterling in two years does not look much like success. Why then cannot we sell our goods? Because the foreigners will not allow us. They put up tariffs to prevent us. And would they not do so in the case of American goods? Now then, some will ask, how are we to obtain our own share of free-trade? I reply, by the same process as we should adopt in the case of military or naval encroachments. We must fight for it, or threaten to do so. Hostile tariffs are acts of industrial war, and should be resisted by the same means as we employ in the case of invasion. A nation which does not insist upon its rights and is prepared to defend them, will soon have none left. War made upon our industries acts in much the same way as physical warfare. Although men are not shot down in a moment, they are first deprived of their work and afterwards thrust upon the streets to starve. Sudden death may be preferable to a gradual draining of life's vital power by hunger.

To obtain our share of free-trade we have got to fight. We must retaliate. There is no other way Reasoning and example has failed. The weapons of self-defence must be taken up and used in grim earnest. To those who would argue that we cannot retaliate without injuring ourselves, I would in turn ask what is the position of a nation which, in self-defence, sends out ships of war to maintain its rights? Is there not a great chance that one of the ships, which has cost a million sterling, may be sent to the bottom of the sea? To say nothing of the sacrifice of hundreds of precious lives, is not the loss of the vessel a contingency counted upon? But does the expected destruction of a few war ships deter a nation from fighting for its own? It is the future safety which is paid for by the immediate loss. The gain is immeasurably greater than the injury received If a policy of retaliation did inflict immediate loss, it would be more than compensated by the gain of a single year under the better conditions of trade.

We are constantly warned by persons, who profess to fear the coming change in British trade policy—which they scent in the air—that we cannot tax food. These fearful folk cannot be aware of the nonsense they talk. We do tax food, and have always taxed it. Every source of food raised in the United Kingdom is taxed, and that heavily. We speak glibly of the English people never being willing to have their food taxed, while at the same time taxes and rates are paid by the British farmer. When the tax was taken off the foreign corn, it was allowed to remain on the home-grown wheat. And what is far worse, the taxes on the home-raised food have been greatly increased by shifting the burden of the taxation for revenue from the foreigner, in a large degree, to the shoulders of the British agriculturist. We sometimes speak of sweating in connection with the match makers; the tailors and the bakers of London. What of the sweating of the poor British farmer and the low paid agricultural labourer? When we eat bread at 4d. a loaf, etc., do we think what it means to the English food producer? We sweat the English wheat-grower without mercy. We compel him and his labourer to compete with the poor Hindoo who labours in the fields for 6d. a day. What the British farmers and labourers might earn and spend with us in the towns we leave out of count. Bread is said to be cheap. It is nominally low-priced, but what is the real and actual cost of our bread? In reckoning up the full cost of our loaf, we must add the loss of six to seven millions of acres of good English soil which is raising nothing but weeds; half a million of capable agricultural labourers—skilled land artizans—driven from their villages into the crowded towns, and 30,000 ruined farmers. We must also count the cost to the British tax-payer of that portion of our great fleet of warships which is required to safeguard our food on the high seas, and then we may arrive at a somewhat accurate approximation of the real cost of the British loaf.

We import annually about 150 millions sterling of food. The English farmer would raise a large portion of this section of the people's food supply if he had a free-market for his produce like the foreigner. In that case, a better customer would be provided for the manufactured articles of the towns in our own home market. The English food grower demands a measure of justice in this so-called free-trade country, and I believe that it will ere long be conceded to him. A few weeks ago, I had the pleasure of attending and taking part in Lord Winchilsea's Agricultural Conferences in York and Winchester. When I said that it was to the interest of the workers in the towns that the British farmer should have his share of free-trade —a free and untaxed market for his food products, the same as the foreigner enjoyed— the mass of farmers and labourers present raised an enthusiastic shout of approval.

As a means to an end, we could tax anything. To obtain free, or nearly free markets abroad, we could bear a temporary loss. Let no one imagine that bread can be dear again from fiscal laws. Bread has been $11\frac{1}{2}$d a loaf since we abolished the corn law. It has been $8\frac{1}{2}$d. only twenty years ago The Crimean war and the Franco-German wars was the cause of the loaf reaching the prices I have referred to. Tariffs of themselves are powerless to render bread very dear. The world's available supply of wheat is the main arbiter in fixing the price of corn and flour. A return to the heaviest corn duty ever imposed in this country would fail to make the bread as dear as it was immediately after the Franco-German war, when we enjoyed free-imports of wheat and food. In addition to those who say that a policy of retaliation would injure the trade of this country, there are others who assert that the slightest interference, with our present fiscal policy, would inevitably lead to protection. This term is much abused. To define my position I would say that my case is free-trade versus free-imports. Some writers, and would-be-authorities, assume that you cannot urge reform of our existing policy without taking up the position of protection versus free-trade. I think that I have made it clear to you that we have no free-trade, and that the supporters of free-imports are virtually protectionists by keeping our ports open and thus making protection abroad possible and profitable. We are mainly responsible for the hostile tariffs of the world. Concerning protection itself, as it is understood by those who use the word so frequently, I declare such a system to be impossible. Protection in the old sense can never be restored. As well try to roll back the economic development of France, Germany, the United States, the British Colonies, and the progress of the United Kingdom, as seek to restore the self-same protection of the first half of the century. If protection could work in the same manner at the present day as free-importers assert that it did in the past, then the nations of Europe and America would have been ruined long ago

I must just refer to those arm-chair Professors and kid-gloved Doctrinaires who tell us that a large excess of imports over exports is a sign of national prosperity. It is a source of prosperity only to those foreign investors who carry on their profit-mongering amid an industrially decaying and starving people. Dividends paid to them in kind—food and other commodities—which are sold in our market and displace British labour, are gain to them, but a loss to the workers.

Speaking of the taxation of our imports, We are agreed not to tax any raw material we cannot produce, such, for instance, as raw cotton. But how long do you expect to get that commodity untaxed? How long will it be before the Americans require their raw cotton for themselves? Out of the 3,500 millions of lbs. they raise annually, the American manufacturers make up about 1,200 millions of lbs. Whenever they require the remainder to provide more employment for their cotton operatives, an export tax of three or four cents. per lb. will be put on, and then good-bye to our British cotton trade. This is no imaginative condition of things. It has been spoken of in this manner in the American Congress at Washington.

I think, however, that I have conclusively proved to you that unless we enforce our principle of free-trade upon our industrial rivals, or equalise the taxation between the foreign and the home producer, British labour interests will continue to suffer; and go on from the exceedingly bad state of to-day to even worse conditions to-morrow. Great Britain has been indulging in an economic Rip Van Winkle sleep, and in the present awakening, she is discovering that her people are starving from the attempt to carry on their industries on the basis of conditions which have ceased to exist.

In conclusion, let me appeal to you, here in this hall—dedicated to the principle of thorough free-trade—let me appeal to you as part of a city, the centre of three millions of population, connected with a great branch of that textile indus ry which has helped to make British exports famous throughout the world. Let me ask you to throw in the scale of fiscal reform the weight and the influence which Manchester and Lancashire has never failed to give in the cause of the people. I call upon you to help to restore England's workshop, not necessarily to the inflated dimensions of 1872, but to such proportion as would fill our mills, factories, and fields with well-paid and contented workers. This is a great question : a national question, and one which should unite to its support every section of Britain's toiling millions whose voice reverberating through the hall of St. Stephen's would bring measures of justice and fairplay for the products of the British worker. Measures that would not only provide peace and plenty for our teeming population, but place Great Britain in a position of harmonious commercial federation with her Colonies, and advance the cause and extend the principle of free-trade itself.

LABOUR INTERESTS & FREE-IMPORTS.

There is no section of commercial interests so directly menaced by the policy of free-imports as the national labour branch. Free-imports threaten the permanence, the stability, and even the existence of whole hives of labour. Free-imports without free-exports displace home labour, and in many instances fail to provide alternative new employments. Manufacturers, and other producers from the employing section, together with capitalists in general, may transfer their plant and their capital to any part of the world where the economic conditions of labour, and the profitable disposal of the products of labour, are the most promising. The British people have almost innumerable instances of this being done, and in some cases by well-known politicians, who loudly vaunt their service in the workers' interest.

Can the British workman so readily transfer his capital - his labour—to foreign lands? In the nature of the case there must be a very close limit to such power when applied to the masses. The worker must leave his native land, and all the dearly-loved associations of his home and kindred, before he is free to profit, even in a minor degree, by the industrial conditions of other countries. There is, in the workman's case, no range of choice as to where he may go to sell his skill and labour. He must, by the necessities of his mode of living, go to those countries only where wages are paid equal to those in his native country.

In quite other ways the capitalist may move He may go where wages are high, as in the case of the United States, and an almost unlimited home market to hand, or he may decide to engage his capital in Germany and other industrial nations where lower rates of wages and an inferior scale of living, among workmen, prevail. In taking either of these courses, he may still remain in Great Britain and enjoy the profits of his foreign investment in his native district. This contrast of the relative powers of action and choice between the capitalist and the workman, proves in the most conclusive manner that the various displacements of British production and labour, which are caused by the artificial economic trend of the practically premium-giving policy of free-imports, leaves the labour section in an almost helpless condition.

A policy of free-imports, conditional upon free-exports, would not act in this disastrous manner A free entrance to foreign ports would provide ample work for the British people, and such questions as the wholesale and unnatural displacement of English labour would not arise. Small and incidental displacements would occur in the ordinary nature of things, as fashion changed, new inventions introduced, or when labour-saving machinery was pressed into the service of a particular industry ; but the huge and trade-destroying displacement of labour, which has been witnessed in this country during the past few years, could not possibly occur under a system of thorough free-trade, *i.e.*, free-selling in addition to free-buying. Free-selling would yield to the products of British labour and productive enterprise—the advantage of the "Law of Surplus" by rendering it possible to produce greater quantities of commodities to be disposed of in free-markets, and sold at a relatively smaller price.

It is a well understood fact in the manufacturing world that a large market can be supplied with particular articles at a smaller cost than would be the case in producing for a lesser one. A firm could turn out a thousand gross of goods at a much less cost per gross than if one hundred gross was the limit. In the former case, labour would be paid at the same rates, and the quality of the workmanship and the material would be the same, as in the latter instance. The difference in the cost of production per gross between the two orders would consist in the saving in the items of several initial costs, and in the economy of management. As in the case of a firm, so, in a greater degree, is the question of quantity a matter of economic concern for a nation

Free-imports as a policy is like a producer who hastens along to meet his industrial competitor, and, with boastful eagerness and personal egotism, insists that his rival shall enjoy the advantage of the "Law of Surplus" all to himself, while he struggles on under restrictive fiscal burdens which he foolishly imagines injure only his commercial opponent's power of competing. Such an extraordinary delusion as this could only exist in the brains of the British victims of the foreign investors' daily and weekly press. It is too true, that the British people, by their policy of free-imports, made free-selling, a splendid reality to all nations but their own. If free-buying is such an economic advantage as the supporters of free-imports assert it to be, why have not the astute Germans, the clever Frenchmen, or the mill-stone penetrating optical cuteness of the Yankees, perceived the wealth-making power of it? In sad truth, our public men of all shades of politics have much to answer, in ignorantly, or wilfully, leaving the masses of the people in this pitiable delusion. The matter cannot be defended, and a wronged and a misled nation will ere long awake from its dream, and, in the light of the noon-day of common-sense, call its rulers and mis-governors to stern account.

The wage-earners of Great Britain, under the wretched pretence of having cheap food supplied to them, are being defrauded of their rightful share of the profits of their industry. This is easily proved: The foreigner—who understands the science of tariffs much better than the English people—knows that a customs duty paid on any competing article which British merchants export to them, acts as an operation on the margin of the profits of the English producer. In other words, a five shillings duty on a pound's worth of English competing exports, necessitates the sale of the said twenty shillings worth of goods for fifteen shillings, to enable them to clear the tariff.* The five shillings duty goes to the foreign Government, to lighten the taxation of the foreign producer. It will thus be seen that the English producer is mulcted of a quarter of the value of his goods. On the supposition that the home manufacturer obtains seven shillings profit on the pound's worth of goods, five-sevenths of this are immediately confiscated by his foreign customer, who imposed the five shillings tariff. The home manufacturer, finding his profits almost destroyed casts about for some relief. and nothing comes so readily as a proposal for a reduction in the wages of his employees. When, by the power of the men's trade union, this decrease in the wages of the operatives cannot be effected, and when, as frequently happens, his remaining slender profit is turned into a loss by a further increase in the foreign tariff, and he decides to close his works, who are the chief sufferers? The

---

* In proof of this statement, the reader is referred to the instructive financial statement of the great Singer Cycle Company, of Coventry, for 1891, in which a large sum (£6,000) is set aside to defray the extra duties on the current year's cycle trade with the United States of America, which the (then recently-passed) McKinley Act exacted. The same kind of evidence as to who pays the tariff on competing goods is forthcoming in regard to the new French tariff of 1892. In those instances in which the duty was raised on English competing exports, British producers were compelled to sell their goods at reduced rates. This is the way in which both employer and workmen are robbed.

workers, who depend on their weekly earnings, are the greatest losers in all such cases. And when one particular producer fails to compete, it is simply a question of time before the other producers follow his example from grim necessity. Some possess larger capital and superior methods of manufacture than others; while some old firms will hold out longer and continue to lose a larger sum in the hope of better times, or out of regard for the poor workers who look up to them for their daily bread; but sooner or later the stoppage comes.

But in despite of all these disadvantages the workers of the country are told that they possess the priceless boon of cheap bread. Let national labour rise in its solidarity and strength, and emphatically declare that there shall be no further hocus-pocus or economic jugglery in this matter. Bread is dirt-cheap, because the farmer and agricultural labourer at home, and labour's co-workers abroad, are underpaid and are sweated. Sweating is the same whether it is in match-making and shirt-stitching, or wheat and food raising, and an injury to any section of labour is an injustice and a wrong to all. Can the worker in the city be prosperous while his fellow toiler in the country is starving? There has been in the past too great a disregard of the wholeness of labour, and its identity of interests through the endless chain of national industries. The bread question is the centre of the labour problem. So long as the foreign investors and fixed-income party can blind the masses by the cheap bread cry, the bondage and helplessness of labour will inevitably continue. This important section of the subject has been worked out by the writer, in several addresses and essays, and need not be further dealt with here.

It may be asked, in closely pressing for evidence, what the policy of free-imports has really done for the interests of labour? It is instantly replied to by the thick-and-thin supporters of the system—that it has given cheap food and abundance of raw materials at minimum rates for the service of labour at home, and, as a corrollery, great advantages for labour's products in neutral markets abroad. This statement may be challenged in its single parts and in its entirety. Nominally low-priced food may not be, and in the case of the British people is not cheap, when the condition of English agriculture, and the fiscal defencelessness of Great Britain for exacting just treatment for her exports, are taken into strict account. As regards raw materials, which cannot be raised at home, few nations dream of taxing them. And in the case of neutral markets, the industrial rivals of British labour products, having first fully qualified themselves to compete in their own home market, have measurably beat the British at their own door, and are now running them close for the first-place in the non-manufacturing centres of the world. A glance at the foreign trade returns, and the nationality of the traders, will speedily show the truth of this statement.

Take the instances of the Southern American Republics, the dominion of Canada, the Colonies of Australasia. the South African Colonies, and many other places, and the trade done with these countries by England's foreign competitors, and the hollowness of the pretention that free-imports yields great advantages to British products in neutral markets, will be at once apparent. A novice in economics would perceive that the qualified foreign competitor, who has his own market and the untaxed entry to Britain's busy marts, must, by the advantage of the "Law of Surplus" and the favourable conditions of his rivalry, sooner or later obtain the first place in neutral markets.

Turning for a moment from this argumentative side of the question to the dry financial facts of British domestic production and commercial enterprise, the stupendous falling off in the Banking transactions in England for 1891-2 should be seriously considered. During those years the shrinkage in the Banking Clearing Hours Returns reached the enormous total of thirteen hundred millions sterling, and a decrease in business transactions amounting to nearly four millions per day.*

---

* It is interesting and most instructive to learn how the chief commercial competitors of Great Britain, viz., France, Germany, and the United States of America, have fared in their Banking transactions during the same period. From the best sources of information it is made manifest that these industrial nations, when compared with England, have done remarkably well. Such financial prosperity, it is safe to assert, is not essentially due to their protective policies, but largely, if not almost entirely, to the free-markets of Great Britain, and the vast and co equal privileges of trading in the British Colonies and dependences.

This somewhat abnormal curtailment in the national Banking turnover, amounting to about twenty per cent. of the whole, denotes, not simply a restriction in the trading enterprise of the country, but very large retrenchments in the spendings of the people. The chief brunt of this monetary sluggishness is almost certain to fall upon labour in its various faceted and protean forms. Labour being the greatest sufferer, it is therefore most natural to assume that labour is the most concerned in the causes of, and the remedies for, this financial and industrial dyspepsia. Sir Thomas Farrar, speaking at the annual meeting of the Cobden Club, July 1893, said that it was regretable to find that many among the working classes, and numbers of trade-unionists, were hankering after protection. He said, in effect, that it was foolish to endeavour to over-ride the power of economic law by Acts of Parliament The students of British industrial history, however, are able to trace the wise and persistent legislative interference with the crude and brutalising forces of soulless economic law. The latter may work through the lowest labour levels, or in connection with the highest and most civilized forms of toil service, where mind assists and supplants muscle. Those who speak and write most often on the unyielding power of economic law, have *immediate gain* as their end, rather than the humanising and unfolding capacities of the race. Where economic law, working under demoralising environments, falls short, the progressive social law steps in and rescues the powerless toiler from the industrial juggernaut. Economic law can be made to act on lines of enlightened and emancipated labour levels, as well as in crude and semi-barbaric forms of toil.

With regard to protection, it is not true that the workers and trade-unionists desire it in the same sense as the Cobdenites understand the term. They desire and constantly seek protection from the unscrupulous under-cutter in wages, and from the brutalising coercion of the "sweater." They also endeavour by the power of their trade combinations to enforce a trade-union rate-of-wages clause in public contracts. This latter, it is true, is a particular form of protection. It is, if technically exhausted, but the insistance of the principle—that public money should be expended on the basis of the labour level, from which the funds were earned. The contrary, if carried out to its logical sequence, would first employ lower labour levels, and gradually drift to barbarism.

There are some political economists who preach the doctrine, "protect the labour and free the product." The plausibility of this scheme seems reasonable enough at first thought; but its impracticability under British labour conditions soon becomes apparent. It is literally impossible to effectually defend British labour and remove restrictions to its products, either at home or abroad, while the policy of free-imports is maintained. The authors of this economic dictum cannot have given adequate consideration to the real effects of Britain's fiscal system. It is not here a question of free-trade, and the removal of barriers to labour's products, but the giving of free-ports to the surplus competing products of foreign labour, while the outcome of British toil—the commodities made by home labour—are burdened in British markets by local and Imperial taxation, and in foreign marts by protective tariffs. Where then is the freedom for British labour products? If the products of English labour are exceptionally taxed in every market in which they are placed, how is it possible to defend British labour interests? If an undue proportion of the value of British labour products goes in taxation, whether in home taxes or foreign tariffs, what chance has labour, be it never so well organized, to obtain its proper reward? It is useless to argue, as the late Professor Fawcett did, that the products of foreign labour had the taxation of the country of origin to bear. Those burdens were for the maintenance of their own home market and the products sold there. In Great Britain, foreign labour products had an untaxed market, and had, therefore, an advantage conferred upon them which was denied to the British. The demand would be, if economic justice held the sway, same product, same tax

There is one other aspect in connection with labour interests and free-imports which deserves close attention. It is the question of the equation of exchange between British and foreign labour products. No one disputes the fact that some nations possess, by climate, soil, minerals, geographical position, and hereditary skill, enormous advantages in some sections of industry over other countries. It is abundantly clear, that if the nations of the earth would permit the absolute free-exchange of those labour products which climate, soil, and other determining factors best fit each set of peoples to produce most easy and profitably, the equation of exchange between the various industrial wealth of the world would speedily right itself. The outcome of a day's labour in one country might exchange for commodities which would, if made at home, consume time equal to a day and a half. The same, or a similar saving of labour, would be effected by each international participant in the cosmopolitan mart. This true economic mode of exchange in its entirety cannot be effected, because the world is insufficiently advanced in real brotherhood. Each nation is bent upon making itself as independent, as self-subsisting, and as self-sufficing as possible, so that in case of war it may be self-reliant and self-protective. In the meantime, labour's interest and true advancement for mankind is constantly sacrificed.

Great Britain has the power to break down the artificial barriers which foreign countries have erected against British labour products—coal alone excepted—and to enforce the progressive power of the equation of exchange between all labour products. To accomplish this international reform, British labour must be called to electoral arms— to fight for its rights by means of the Ballot Box. Under the present system of free-imports labour is helpless, and Great Britain impotent to free-labour products. Labour, wielding the greater part of the electoral strength of the state, is no longer powerless to guide the legislative helm, but may, if wise counsels prevail, not only rescue the industrial interest of the toiling millions from the perilous condition in which they are placed, but save England herself from the loss and disgrace of sinking in the scale of nations.

Equality of Taxation, or Free-Markets for British products, at home and abroad, are the just demands of the British producer.

FREE-SELLING IN ADDITION TO FREE-BUYING.

"TO ENFORCE, NOT FORSAKE, FREE-TRADE."

A Speech delivered in the Exchange, Wolverhampton, April 23rd, 1892.

My object this evening is to endeavour to prove, by strict reference to the industrial development of the chief nations of the world, and the treatment of British exports, that the time has come for the compulsory enforcement of free-trade between Great Britain and her international customers. To enforce, and not forsake the practice of free-trade is the fiscal need of the time, and my advocacy this evening has no other purpose in view. My opponents, however, would have you believe that the contrary is the case, and that I am in opposition to free-trade itself, and desire the British people to return to protection. This foolish conviction on their part is a singular proof of the warping power of an unreasoning belief in a popular term, which blinds them to the fact of the non-fulfilment of the conditions which are essential to the existence of free-trade in any shape.

Reference has been made to the non-party character of this meeting. Some persons regard a discussion of this subject as being one particularly associated with Conservatives. Speaking for myself, I am a Radical in politics, and at the present time a Radical Labour Candidate for one of the Parliamentary constituencies in my own town of Birmingham ; and, so far as I am personally concerned, I would prefer that this question were a Radical party question, so that that party should continue in a policy which I consider one of its best traditions —the interests and welfare of the masses of the working classes of the country. It is not a party question, but it is a great question. It is a question of real free-trade, and not the sham we have been accustomed to now for so many years.

Now in the course of the remarks I shall have the pleasure to address to you, I shall endeavour to occupy your time as profitably as possible, and give you such facts and figures which will enable you to estimate the importance of the subject which is somewhat complex and difficult that is, when you do not understand it —and if you will only carefully consider this question—the commercial policy of the country —and see how it affects you working people, you will very soon recognise how important it is that it should be brought before those who are responsible for your well-being. I gave seven years hard study to this question before I came to a definite opinion, as I did not wish to make any false move in public, and I ultimately came to this conclusion—that the great principles of free-trade advocated by Cobden, Villiers, Thompson, and Bright, had been lost sight of. You know that in the old days, the agitation for cheap food for the people led to the abolition of the Corn Laws, and from that time the question of free-trade was a great question with the Liberal party. The essential features of that question was to promote goodwill between nation and nation, and the free-exchange of all articles of commerce. That we all admit was an admirable policy, and one which we could all endorse. But in comparing the practice of this country in its commercial relations with others, I found the most important features of the question forgotten and neglected, and while we were giving what is called free-trade to other nations they were absolutely doing all they could to prevent us getting any benefit in return. From 1849, when the great tax of the old Corn Laws was taken off, till 1874, we had gradually taken off tax after tax, and from that year we entered upon what is called a full free-trade programme, and so far as we were concerned, the only taxes which were retained were those on articles which we could not produce. I wish to make my position perfectly clear. I am to-night still a free-trader, a real free-trader, free on both sides, believing that as a principle there is nothing like it—believing there is no better object in the interests of the country than in the promotion of its trade. But what have we seen to be the result of the policy which has ruled the Governments of this country for years past? That our generosity has been traded upon by the great commercial rivals of Great Britain, and that the meanest advantage has been taken by other nations of the position in which we have placed ourselves. Take the case of America. Every year we send less and less of our full labour productions in consequence of the heavy restriction they impose upon them, and it is in fact almost a difficulty to sell at all, whilst they are sending us their own productions in increasing quantities every year. What does all this mean ? That what you are paying America for, in many things represents the wages the working men ought to get in our own country, where a burden is borne of ninety millions of taxation annually, for the purpose of its maintenance. We have made many efforts to endeavour to persuade other nations as to the justice of our commercial principles, notably, by the force of example. But what reply have you received ? Not only have other nations refused to recognise the value of these concessions made to them in our trading policy, but have actually done all they could to make the burdens on British trade heavier than before.

Still the cry goes on among those who benefit by our present policy, that it is for the good of the country, a cry which is re-echoed by the whole press. They say that the foreigners are fools to tax themselves as they do, and that though they perhaps think they injure us, they hurt themselves still more. But has it ever occurred to you to ask whether there is any purpose in all this ; whether other nations are such blockheads to carry on such a system which is said to be so ruinous to their own interests. It seems strange that we alone of all nations on the face of the globe, should persist in a policy quite adverse to that of others— let them borrow our capital, get our foremen to teach their own people the secrets of our trade, and teaching them to make goods to flood our markets, thus making a huge warehouse of England, whilst our own people are walking about seeking employment. Doesn't it seem strange to you that such a state of things should exist if this policy of free-trade is the great benefit it is said to be ? But I will tell you what I have found out whilst calmly considering the reasons which prevent those, who should know, recognizing the importance of the subject —that our members of the House of Commons are ignorant, and that the entire press of the country is ignorant. These are stupendous facts, but are nevertheless true. I have, in fact, written private letters to some of the leading papers in the country, pointing out the most serious mistakes they have made in articles published on this subject, but they are intimately linked up together in this state of things that makes England the warehouse of the goods of other nations instead of being the great manufacturing centre it ought to be. I know perfectly well that we cannot give up buying foreign goods altogether—we don't want to. We are too much imbued with the principles of free-exchange to deny the foreigner the privilege or the opportunity of sending us what we wish to buy. But when they take our capital, our machinery, our best workmen, and copy our ideas, we do claim the right that they shall give us the same privilege in exchange for our productions in their own markets, from which we are now partially excluded. I have said before, we are driven to no other conclusion than that the leading politicians of this country are hoodwinking the people to continue in a position which they know is in favour of their own interests—that is, the interest of the capitalist class. They will point out to you certain statements to prove their own case, but I know something about the relative value of the information to be obtained, and I say this, that we in England are far worse off than other nations in regard to statistical facts. I say far worse because you really don't know where you are. There are no detailed facts or figures from which to accurately judge your position. So far as I am able to judge— and I am speaking on a subject which I have for years carefully studied—the facts and figures that are available have been so carefully prepared so as to blind you as far as possible to the trade of the country. What will they do to start with—I mean those who support the present policy of free-imports? They will try to show you and impress upon you the grandeur of the merchant maritime power of England, for the purpose of pointing out the amount of our national commerce in value. That is right enough—I am not opposed to all this. But what I do say, is that the value does not represent our productions, and if we are simply to become a carrying nation for the goods of others instead of producers, we are not providing a means of employment for our working people, in the sense those who urge this as an argument, wish to convey.

In 1851, two years after the free-trade policy had been adopted, we exported three million tons of coal. You know the value of that article with which we in this country have been blessed by providence with a superabundance. It is to trade, what the spade and the plough is to the farmer. Well, since that period the exports in this alone have gone on increasing, and the quantity annually exported is something like thirty million tons. We are not jealous of selling our coal, but we do object when it is employed in other countries to make our iron, to make our steel, to make our girders—all of which we formerly made and sold abroad—the very coal you are sending away you ought to be working with here. I have been in the North of England, and I know the intelligence of the miners of Durham and Northumberland, who live on a hard and hazardous occupation. But there would not be so many sons of miners as there are following the same occupation as their fathers were there other opportunities for employment. But they have been forced to remain where they are. There are 613,000 men and boys in that industry. They dig up the coal and sell it to France, for instance, and France is sending it back in the shape of manufactured goods which ought to be made by our own workpeople. I don't care what any Liberal or Conservative thinks of it—both parties seemed to be able to grasp at one idea only. Their one cry to other nations is to produce, produce, produce, but here they say to us, consume, consume, forgetting the fact that you must produce before you are able to consume. What is the use of telling me or anyone else that such a policy as this will not find its own level in time. But they will tell you that if you tax your imports of manufactured goods you must also tax your loaf. But you do tax your loaf—that is, the corn grown at home —by so heavily taxing the owners and workers of land, who grow some of your food. I am not specially in favour of the landlords of this country. I am opposed to many of the privileges they enjoy. Quite apart from this subject, I say that the food raised on the land, the agricultural land, is taxed to death. I am not referring to such land as the Duke of Westminster has got in London, where miles and miles of streets produce him an immense income purely from the accident of circumstances. I speak of the man who tills the English soil, the most fertile in the world—a soil on which ought to be raised two-thirds of your food—and say that such land should be taxed as little as possible, and that the landlord should not be allowed to put the difference into his own pocket by means of an increased rent. There will be such a thing in the near future as a Land Court for the English farmer. But let no man dream that the landlords will reap all the value of the difference. With the power of the franchise in their possession, the people of this country would never allow that to take place, but would see that whatever reductions were made should be devoted to the benefit of the man who is directly responsible for the cultivation of the land. From a statement made in 1885, it appears that the tax on agricultural land was 12s. per acre, whilst in America it is only 6d. This was why the American, the Russian, and other people could place their wheat on the English market, and undersell our own produce. I say that all food should be as free as air, but as a matter of fact you do tax the food that is raised here.

Of course, the Chancellor of the Exchequer must have a revenue, but I do object, and I believe the people will object in a more forcible manner before long, to the compulsion to contribute the whole necessary amount, and allow the foreigner, who makes such good use of our markets to go free. What reason is there that import duties should not be placed upon foreign manufactured goods coming here? Take the case of France who sends annually seven million pounds worth of manufactured silks to this country, when it might as well be done here and provide employment for a large population. I know there are some classes who use silk, but only those who can afford it, and yet it pays no tax at all, when it comes into our markets and displaces our own productions. Now I would not mind that, if France would allow our goods to go into their country free. But no. She has put more and more taxes upon our goods whilst she has an absolutely free market here. We have to raise £90,000,000 annually to maintain the services, which other nations do not contribute anything towards, but are at the same time driving us out of our own markets. There is a saying, you know, that they "manage things better in France," and they certainly appear to do so in this matter of trade. She raises her revenue from those who sell in her markets, grants government monopolies, but takes good care not to touch the food of the people any more than is really necessary.

I am for the taxation of land in towns. That is a very different thing from taxing the land which grows the food of the people. Unless I make a mistake, there is about to be a return of the people to the land of England. In consequence of that agitation which has existed for some time and is going on, I believe the people are gradually going back to the land when facilities are completed for easily obtaining small holdings of about ten acres. The cultivation of the land for the people by the people is a principle which I believe will have great influence upon this question. What we want is a few more million landlords or land-hirers, and then you will see the last day when there will be much taxation on land which is cultivated for the purpose of providing food for the people.

If the French and Germans have a free market here, then let us have a free market in return ; and if they will not yield it, we shall have to find means to enforce a solution, and make them recognize our principle in this matter by placing a small tariff on their manufactured goods. You will no doubt say that all this is very well, but that I have not given you many facts. Oh yes, I can. I should not believe in a remedy if I could not. It is all very well for a politician to come and give you his opinion on various subjects, but on this question we must have something more than that. How are we going to do it ? In comparing the relative increase and decrease of our imports and exports we find an increase of £15,000,000 in the imports. But they don't give you money for the goods you send abroad—they send you manufactured goods in payment. If you get the Board of Trade returns, you will see that during 1890, that £63,000,000 of fully manufactured goods were imported into this country from foreign nations, and £65,000,000 in 1891. And so the merry game goes on ; at the same time the foreigner is putting more and more burdens upon our own productions. The result was that large mills were standing still, and thousands upon thousands of men and women idle. I say again, you have been kept in the dark on this question, you have been befooled; the entire press of the country have entered into a conspiracy to put these things before the people in a wrong way, urging that cheapness was their motto. You are concerned, and I am concerned, in the amount of work done in our mills, especially when you reflect upon the importance of the fact that £65,000,000 of manufactured goods are sent into this country which our own people could make. Steel rails, tin ware, iron girders and other things that were formerly made here and sent to foreign markets are now brought in here free, and that policy is supported by the press on the ground that it is cheap. What is the use of having things cheap if you have no money to buy them? And if you have money, goods cannot be dear. But how are you going to get it if you allow other nations a free hand to take away our own commerce, and throw people out of employment? The first and last consideration of all is for work wherewith to produce your wages, and good wages too.

Now let me tell you at this point what the other nations of the world have been doing. We have been tricked into the position we are now in, by the ungenerous advantage taken of our free-importing policy. The foreigners know perfectly well that it would be against their interests to adopt a policy like that we have in England Nothing will change them in that. They don't believe in free-trade, and it answers their purpose admirably for this country to continue in its present course in regard to its commercial relations. After we had entered upon a commercial policy of free-imports for all competing goods, which did not take place until 1874, Bismarck was the first to take special advantage of it. In 1879, finding most of the German furnaces down, mills idle, and large numbers of his countrymen out of work, he said "This will not do." What did he do? Why, he simply went to the German Parliament and raised the tariffs against other nations, to protect German native industries and find employment for the people. You must bear in mind that these high tariffs do not touch other nations like they do us. I will give you a case to illustrate what I mean. The new French tariff which came into operation early in the year 1892, nearly doubled the duty on cycles going into France. We alone are injured by this increase of tariff, because we are the only nation which exports cycles in quantities. Yes, they almost doubled the tariff; and they not only effectually protect and encourage their manufacture in their own country, but you will find that before many years are passed that they will be sending cycles over here, and under-selling our own makers.

I am not a protectionist. I am opposed to unfair protection in every conceivable form; but this is the position we are now in—so long as other nations can depend upon our markets being open for them, they will continue to put fresh duties upon our exports. We are indeed the protectionists, since we encourage and permit other countries to tax us Our free markets alone make it profitable. If, therefore, we were in a position to put a tax on their imports, you would find that they would think twice before they took any steps, which would ultimately recoil upon themselves John Stuart Mill, one of the best and most widely recognized authorities on political economy of later years, said that the only way by which a nation can prevent loss by taxation by tariffs is to place a similar tax on others in return. But we do nothing, and matters are allowed to drift on in the old sweet way. What is the reason ? The class of men who now represent you in Parliament have, as a rule, plenty of money. They can take their money anywhere ; they can take their capital anywhere ; but the British working man is compelled to stay at home. Look at Mundella's case, at Saxony, when he took part of his industry there for the purpose of getting the work done cheaper, and sent here free. It was the same with Jacoby, of Nottingham, who went with his machinery to make lace curtains and hosiery in Germany, whilst his own workmen were standing idle and starving. How is it that Liberals and Free-Traders do not raise their voices against such instances as these ? Bismarck has raised his voice against such a policy in regard to German industries, and here we find ourselves completely surrounded by an almost impregnable wall of hostile tariffs, and do nothing to attempt to destroy it. If you don't get work you don't get wages, and if you don't get wages you starve. In 1881 France had a large measure of free-trade with us, but her Government would not renew the Treaty when it had expired, and it is officially given on the authority of Sir Joseph Crow, who was specially commissioned to inquire into the matter in France, that our trade with that country since that period had fallen from £28,000,000 to £21,000,000, an annual loss of nearly £7,000,000. In the United States our trade is losing ground in alarming proportions, and since the operation of the McKinley Tariff Act, which raised the average duties from 41 to to 52 per cent., the position has become more serious. Not only this, but a similar policy was adopted by other countries. Belgium followed, Canada followed, Austria followed, in fact, they all followed ; and here is England, the only country in the world with a commercial policy ruinous to our native industries, and in favour of the foreigner. As I have said, they all raised their tariffs, because so long as we allowed them a free market here we are actually giving them a premium to send their manufactured goods here and to tax ours. If we desired at the present time to take steps to prevent this hostile feeling by way of checking it, you would find these foreigners would not be so anxious to increase their duties if England stepped in and said, " If you don't reduce your taxes on our manufactures going into your markets, we shall tax your goods coming into ours, and so we warn you." A policy of retaliation would have stopped much of the excessive duties now levied, and it is for you, working men and the people of the country, to give the matter full consideration in time, before all your trade is taken from you by foreigners

I am perfectly well aware that some people object to a policy of coercing other nations to act fairer to English trade. But you can do no good without the power of compulsion. Of what use would a national system of education be if it were not for compulsion? It was in urging a policy of compulsion that Mr. Gladstone spoke on the Land Purchase Bill. So if you want to show your power to other nations in this question of trade you must show that you not only have the power to retaliate, but intend to exercise that power. I do not object to a moderate duty, say of ten per cent., because I have so much faith in British skill and enterprise, and the ability of our own workmen, that we should not be barred to a very great extent from competing with our goods in other countries. But when you come to forty, fifty, and sixty per cent., it is time for the Government to take decided action.

Hostile tariffs are equivalent to an act of war, and if you are not prepared to protect your own interests you must eventually lose. If free-trade is such a good thing as we are told it is, how is it that our example is never followed? You don't find any country following our example—as a matter of fact the tendency is all the other way—so that it makes you think that we cannot have all the sense, and that there must be reasons for other nations to continue in the course they have adopted. Do you think they would be so blind to their own interests to keep up these high tariffs unless it paid them to do so ? Would they not rather obtain a revenue by some other means, if they believed it would be better for them to do so ? But no. They know better. They make the foreigner contribute his share of their national charges, and so relieve their own shoulders from a too excessive burden This policy of free-trade is, of course, supported by the capitalist class in this country, because it enables them to invest their money abroad—the money they have got out of your labour. What we want to do is to encourage British capital to remain at home. The fact is that members of Parliament do not understand the matter They may come down here, as one of your own members did a short time ago, and make very good speeches on certain lines, but when you come to appeal to them on the subject of British trade they know nothing about it. You want work and you want wages, but you cannot get them so long as the present commercial system of the country remains as it is, because you are handicapped so heavily by the foreigner that we cannot make any impression. You must demand from your representatives in Parliament that they shall support some measure which will enforce foreign nations to give us the same privileges of free-trade that we give to them.

Take the state of our exports for the year 1891. They fell off $18\frac{3}{4}$ millions sterling. No wonder that you are walking the streets starving. Now let us just consider in what class of goods the exports declined in. Cotton and textile fabrics fell off from 112 to 106 millions sterling, and metal of all kinds, raw and manufactured, from 45 to 39 millions sterling, and machinery from 16 to about 15 millions sterling. These make up 13 millions sterling out of the 18¾, and you working men, in Wolverhampton here, can easily understand how a shrinkage of six millions in metals in one year can affect you. I know that you are told that it is not all in consequence of hostile tariffs that our exports have declined, but from other causes—such, for instance, as the failure of the Baring Bros , in the Argentina affairs. But even this is an indirect outcome of the tariff war, which makes it unprofitable for English capitalists to employ their money at home in British industry. What capitalist would desire to risk his money in foreign countries, and bran-new Republics, even at the highest rate of interest, where in the nature of things he can exercise little or no control over the government of such lands, if he could employ it profitably in his own country? The essence of the question lies in this matter of foreign investments, and any difficulty which arises from time to time, on account of recklessness or extravagance in the use of English funds, is only another way of showing the unwisdom of producing abroad, instead of employing our own people at home. Look at the way in which your money, saved from the labour of past years, has been expended in the Argentine Republic—the great Republic of South America, great only in almost limitless barren acres and crushing indebtedness. A revenue of five millions, and a debt of 120 millions or thereabouts. Just think of these people spending your hard-earned money in building an Opera House as grand as the French Opera Palace in Paris, and a Stock Exchange building, costlier than our Exchange in London, and great palatial banking houses, and other public institutions. This is partly why you are starving now in this good old hard-working town.

I appeal to the masses of the people to take this question up in their own interests. Those who ought to represent us, but do not, have gone too deep in the rut of party to alter their course, and they will never give enough consideration to these matters, which are of so much importance that they affect the very vitals of the nation. Men of Wolverhampton, those of you who know what it is to walk about idle, week after week, whilst you see the very goods you ought to make coming from abroad and draining the country of its wealth, rend assunder all party ties in viewing this trade question. I now appeal to the working men of Wolverhampton—typical of the toiling masses of Great Britain—to arrest the progress of industrial decay which has set in upon the vital trades of the nation. Concentrate your minds with a singleness of purpose upon the productive industries of the country—the means by which you work and live, and the true source of

England's national wealth. Be not led from this point by the account of the shipping tonnage, which has grown from $6\frac{1}{2}$ to 8 million tons during the past ten years, or to the volume or value of our total exports and imports Dwell rather upon the appalling facts that there are about a million men and women unemployed in the country, another million of paupers, and a paupers' annual bill of $10\frac{3}{4}$ millions sterling. Point to the millions of acres of good English soil which has been driven out of cultivation, and to tens of thousands of farmers who have been wrecked and ruined, and to the hundreds of thousands of agricultural labourers who have been forced from their native villages into the already over-crowded towns Think of those facts, and demand a remedy from your representatives. The future position and civilization of the British race demands immediate measures of reform in this mighty question of international commerce Work and wages for the people, and justice to British exports should be your political battle cry. Don't be deceived by a cry of cheap imports, refer to the fact that you are being undersold in your own markets by those who do not contribute one penny towards your national exchequer in the way of taxes. Appeal to the fact that you want no more than justice, and that, while you believe still in the commercial greatness of England, you know that it is only by changing our policy that we can avoid the dangers to which it leads, and enable her to maintain her position in the vanguard of civilization.

WHY I OPPOSE THE POLICY OF FREE-IMPORTS

A Speech delivered in Birmingham, March 12th, 1890.

In appearing before a Birmingham audience as a critic and opponent of the national fiscal policy of free-imports, inaccurately named free-trade, I deem a few remarks in explanation of my position to be necessary.

As a life-long Liberal, I have, until the last seven years, believed it to be my duty to support our existing policy, on the ground of its many commercial, industrial and social advantages. My belief in the boasted benefits of free-trade was rudely shaken when Prince Bismarck raised a protective tariff against British competing exports in 1879 – which was increased in 1885 — and France refused to renew the Cobden treaty in 1881. The new French treaty,* which the British Government was compelled to sign, raised the tariff still higher against English goods. The Canadian Parliament, the Belgium Government, and other countries followed the example of

---

* This treaty was notoriously unfair in its bearing upon British and French commercial interests. Numerous classes of French goods were admitted to British markets duty free, while a limited number of English articles were permitted to enter French ports at a reduced tariff. It is well-known to British producers how the inroad of French goods, under the treaty,—notably watches, ribbands and silks—almost ruined the trade of Coventry, Macclesfield and other places without equivalents in larger exports to France as a set-off. The hope existed of converting France to free-trade, and by that example the rest of Europe. How all expectations in this respect have been falsified is now the stalest of historical facts. For full details concerning the effects of this treaty, the reader is referred to Mr. R. A. Macfie's work—" Cries in a Crisis"—published in 1881.

Germany and France, and set up protective tariffs against British and Irish exports. This set me thinking concerning the nature of free-trade, and how far a policy of free-imports yielded any free-trade at all. Great Britain, I saw, was powerless to prevent even a most flagrant breach of the free-trade system by her great industrial rivals, and I knew that our policy of free-imports at-any-price stood condemned. I looked to the leaders of Liberalism for some sign of reform in the matter, but none was made. In its absence, however, there was plenty of foolish abuse of foreign statesmen, concerning their reactionary policy, but not a solitary sentence regarding the need of the reajustment of our trading system to meet the altered fiscal policy of the entire world. My course became clear. Since Liberals, as a party, would not move, the duty of individual initiative, in the way of reform, seemed to me to be imperative, and I come before you to-night, after seven years thoughtful consideration of the subject, to make my first effort on behalf of real free-trade, and justice to British labour. Having resolved to take this course, from a sternly conscientious sense of individual duty, as a citizen of this important industrial, centre, I shall not mind what political associates or townsmen may think, so long as I win the thoughtful approbation of a few earnest minds, who I hope will form the nucleus of a reforming party. Having made these personal observations, perhaps you will permit me to say a little on the general aspects of the subject.

Great Britain is peculiarly situated as regards the industrial question. In the first place, she has to provide labour to a very densely crowded population, numbering nearly 500 to the square mile. To rightly guage our position in this respect we have but to refer to France, with her 38 millions of population, which have a density of 187 to the square mile ; to Germany, with 40 millions of inhabitants, and 226 to the mile ; to Italy, with her 30 millions, and a density of 240 ; and to the United States of America, with their 60 millions of citizens, and the extremely small number of 20 to the square mile. Even the old Empire of China, with her 300 to 400 millions of people, has a density of population less than one half that of Great Britain. It will thus be clearly perceived that we must have plenty of labour and a mighty trade with which to employ our people. Small sections of commerce will not suffice. The crumbs which fall from the world's industrial table will not feed Britain's teeming millions. In the next place we have to consider the weighty fact that the agriculture of Great Britain has been systematically neglected, unjustly treated, and, as a consequence, partially ruined. Half-a-million skilled farm labourers have been driven from their native villages, and thirty thousand farmers ruined during the last forty years. The unnatural supremacy of manufacture during the best half of this century has been the potent cause of the degradation of the nation's great farming interest. At the present time the proportion of the agricultural industry, to the total of industries of the country, is but 14 per cent. In France and Germany it is 26 and 32 per cent. This state of things constitute a national peril An industrial and social nemesis follows closely on our commercial track, and will, unless I miscalculate the forces of reaction, bring industrial wreck and semi-starvation to to the masses of this country. The signs are ominous, and I prophesy a dire condition of misery and distress to the working classes of the country in the near future, unless British statesmen demand a large measure of free-trade for English exports.

You have not, up to the present time, felt very much of the effects of our suicidal policy, because our foreign rivals have not fully supplied their own home wants. Whenever they have accomplished that part of their industrial development, you may expect the full force of their competition, both in your own and in the neutral markets of the world. You are practically powerless to resist them, since you permit them to tax your exports by hostile tariffs, and also yield them a free and untaxed market here for their surplus commodities. Weigh well what I state to you. I say that industrial ruin threatens as an approaching doom, and as a direct consequence of your blind adherence to the party cry of free-trade. No free-trade exists, and the present policy is a sham and a delusion, which the people have foolishly worshipped, ignorantly believing it to be free-trade.

In all the varied aspects of the case, there is none so instructive as that of the world's imitation of all the mechanical inventions and industrial methods of Great Britain, and its strict refusal to adopt the policy of free-trade. They, the nations of the earth, have almost slavishly copied everything that has contributed to our wealth and greatness, but they, one and all, reject our free-trade policy. This striking fact should set us thinking about our policy, and of the prospects for our future. It is seldom if ever, that the collective wisdom of mankind—the British nation excepted—should be in the wrong.

Another important feature of the case is the common belief that the commercial, industrial, and social progress during the last forty years is due to the policy of free-imports—falsely named free-trade. A greater falsehood and a more pernicious delusion were never before foisted upon a too credulous people. It is abundantly clear at this latter date that, the nation has developed in spite of free-imports, and not as a consequence of such policy. The extension of the Railway system, the discovery of gold in Australia and Calatornia, the new processes in the making of steel, the wars in which our commercial rivals were engaged, and many other things contributed to the extraordinary prosperity of Great Britain, and, in fact, were the only causes of our commercial progress. As a proof that the policy of free-imports was not the parent of our industrial growth, I have simply to refer to the commercial development of France, Germany, and the United States of America, during the same period. These countries have pursued the opposite fiscal policy to that which we have adopted. They have been protectionist. Have they failed, as our over-wise political economists asserted that they would do? No, they have not! but on the contrary—they have succeeded, relatively, greater than Great Britain, and that in despite of the drawback of great wars. If there is any power in logic, it must be apparent that if a given policy is the cause of national progress, its absence must imply non-progress How, then, did France, Germany, and the United States, succeed? Not in consequence of free-imports, because no such policy existed. It is manifest from the history of these countries that they have a better show of fact and reason for asserting that they have progressed on account of their respective policies of protection, than we have for our contention. It is, however, more likely that the cause of their industrial and commercial advancement, like our own in the past, was mainly due to the adoption of great inventions and superior methods of production.

I think that you will now see with me the necessity for the reajustment of our international trade policy to suit the needs of the time, and the world's concurrent advancement, and not with an air of superior wisdom, dogmatically assert the benefits of our own policy and the foolishness of our trade rivals. It is high time that we examined the present-day foundations of our economic theories.

It is said with a tone of national pride that we have cheap bread. Yes. Cheap bread, and a starving peasantry. Cheap bread, and the wail of agricultural distress. Cheap bread, and heavy taxation to build ships of war to safeguard our food supply on the high seas. Cheap bread, and six millions of England's broad acres growing weeds.

There are many sides of this question which I would like to bring before your notice, but I must leave them to future occasions. We have heard so much of the national benefits of free-imports. But what of the disadvantages and the disasters attending the policy? It is well to look after the interests of the consumer, but has the producer no rights? All workers must produce before they can consume. The producer's side of the case cannot be neglected or sacrificed without peril to the country's wealth-producing power. When a nation ceases its production, it permits the source of its prosperity and greatness to depart.

As an example of the disadvantageous economic trend of our international commercial exchange under the policy of free-imports, I will give you the average quantities of goods sent to us from the United States, France, Germany, and Russia, during the last nine years, and the amount of commodities which these countries took from us in exchange. The United States sent us goods to the value of £2 9s. 9d. per head of our population, and received from us in return the small amount of 10s. 3d. per head of their population. Taking into account the difference in our respective populations, the Americans took less than one half the goods in return than they should have done. France is almost as bad. She sent us £1 1s 8d. per head of our population, and took in exchange 8s. 3d. per head of her inhabitants. The population in this case being nearly equal. Germany follows, with goods to us representing 13s. 9d. per head, and takes in return but 7s. 4d. per inhabitant. Russia ships us goods to the value of 9s. 9d. per head of the British population, and receives in exchange from this country exports to the amount of 1s. 3d. per head of her own people. After making allowance for the great disparity of the population of the two countries, Russia takes less than one half of our manufactured goods in payment for her exports to us, which reacts as a distinct loss to our productive industry.

It is true that we import cheap food, but in the wake of the policy which permits the wheat sweepings of the world to be landed on our shores, I see ruined and deserted villages, and the gaunt spectres of British farmers who have been driven from the farms and the homesteads of their fore-fathers, starving in the midst of plenty. I also see the goods which have been made by British workmen, blocked in foreign ports by hostile tariffs, or sold for two-thirds their value to the ruin of the British manufacturer, and the loss of employment to the workers I have forced upon my attention the unjust competition of foreign goods, which are sold in our markets without contributing a single penny to the cost of our Government, while the British manufacturer, like the English farmer, is taxed to death. I think of the labour which the people need or they starve I ask, Where are our future markets, either at home or abroad? What of the future of Great Britain and the British Empire? Shall the blind and fanatical attachment to a mere phrase stand in the way of Britain's onward march? No! no! a thousand times no! The present system must be firmly set aside, and an economically sound policy substituted—one that will meet the just and necessary demands of England's labour army, and the industrial and economic needs of the country.

Although the policy of free-imports be encased in the triple armour of vaunted trade-freedom, plausibility, and half-century assertions, it shall be pierced and decimated by the logic of hostile tariffs, and the unanswerable arguments of our defeated industries and commercial decline; and the producers—the mainstay of England's commercial greatness—shall be placed in a position of real productive freedom, alike as regards foreign competitors, neutral markets, and the true interest of British home consumers themselves.

FREE-TRADE WITHOUT FREEDOM.

FREE-IMPORTS

(A DELUSIVE PORTION OF FREE-TRADE)

LEAVES BRITISH COMMERCE DEFENCELESS AGAINST THE OVER-PRODUCTION AND HOSTILE TARIFFS OF THE WHOLE WORLD.

Open Letter to the Most Hon. the Marquis of Salisbury.

MY LORD,—To you, as a responsible Statesman, I beg to submit the following observations concerning our national fiscal policy :—

The policy of free-trade (which has never extended beyond the present system of partial free-imports) has, by the commonly-assumed consent of the majority of the electors, been the chosen fiscal arrangement for our commercial transactions with the outside world. This system has been maintained, and persisted in, despite the world's cold and collective rejection of it, under the mistaken belief that the great social and industrial advantages enjoyed by the people, during the last forty years, were the direct results of its wealth-bestowing power.

The British people have seen their mechanical inventions and business methods, and even their progressive plans of government, taken up one after another, initiated and adopted, by foreign nations ; but to their extreme surprise and complete repulse, the great fiscal policy on which they believed their prosperity rested, has been openly and repeatedly repudiated. This conduct on the part of the wealth-seeking industrial countries, has caused many electors to seriously examine the whole question of free-trade, as practised by the English nation, and as a result of the unbiased investigation, a great change of opinion on the subject has taken place. The central fact, which has slowly but unmistakably forced itself upon their minds, is, that a policy of free-trade, with one party only to the bargain, is commercial and fiscal madness, and must inevitably end in national ruin. The day of reckoning, however, has at length arrived. The working class electors are putting the economic theories in support of free-imports (free-trade is not in question, as it does not exist) to the rigid test of common-sense, *and discarding blind belief and party-ties, are asking plain questions, which require equally plain answers.* The following express in brief the main drift of their enquiries :—

1st. Why have we, the wealthiest and the most skilled manufacturing people in the world, a million and a half of workers idle, and a vast number but partly employed?

2nd. Why do we—who bear annually 142 millions sterling of imperial and local taxation—import, free of duty, 65 millions sterling of manufactured articles, and 50 millions sterling of wheat and flour, when we might make the larger part of the former, and raise and mill the best portion of the latter ourselves?

3rd. Why are the great industrial nations taking less and less of our fully-manufactured articles, and sending us more and more of theirs?

4th. Why do we import wheat from Russia, tea from China, and raw cotton from the United States of America—who prevent profitable trade with them by their hostile tariffs—when India, Canada, and Australasia could soon raise the whole?

5th. Since the United States of America have developed so enormously under the influence of internal free-trade within their vast territory, is it not time for the British Empire (which has three times the extent) to fiscally federate and do likewise?

6th. Is it not politically criminal to blindly adhere to a policy which has, in the logical sequence of events, almost destroyed our agriculture, comparatively restricted our trade, and rapidly finishing what it has already begun—the commercial alienation of our great Colonies?

7th. Has John Bull become such an imbecile, or so much in the power of the British foreign investors and middle-men importers, that he cannot reverse or modify a policy which the united wisdom of mankind rejects; a policy which robs him of the power to make the best of his own Empire, and which opens the door to the pauperization of his own people?

Between the years 1850 and 1890, France and the United States of America (protectionist countries) have increased their total national wealth about 150 per cent., per head of their respective populations, while England, with her boasted free-trade (not free-trade, but free-imports only) has increased hers 25 per cent.—a comparative decline. Abolish sham free-trade with the outside world, and commence real free-trade relations with the Empire

FREE-TRADE A LIVING SHAM.

A REJECTED POLICY BY ALL THE WORLD

A COLONIAL TRADE UNION
TO SECURE EXTENDED MARKETS AND HIGHER WAGES
IS ENGLAND'S ONLY CHANCE.

Open Letter to the Right Hon. William Ewart Gladstone.

RESPECTED SIR,—I humbly submit the following statements to your consideration :—

Free-Trade is a dishonoured title while the markets of the world are blocked to British goods.

Free-Imports open our ports to the over-productions of our manufacturing rivals, and deprives the British workman of his rightful labour.

Free-Imports leave no margin to the British people to make advantageous trade treaties with friendly nations, or to give favoured terms to our Colonies and and possessions—favoured terms that would develop the resources of our Empire, and render us an imperial trades union.

Free-Trade has outlived its splendid prophecies, and is a corpse tied round the neck of John Bull, who struggles manfully with his crushing burden.

Free-Trade says "Buy in the cheapest markets," which is an immoral doctrine, since it floods our markets with the products of the sweaters of Europe, who force their hands to labour 70 hours a week. Ask trade-unionists if cheap labour is moral?

Free-Imports have given us cheap bread by attracting the surplus wheat of the world, and has materially assisted to ruin our agriculture, and has driven millions of acres out of cultivation, and half-a-million farm labourers into our over-crowded towns.

Free-Trade, by giving away all its favours, has tempted foreign countries into the selfish but calculating policy of blockading British goods by heavy tariffs.

Free-Imports have driven British capitalists, with English machinery, to foreign lands, where trade is fostered, leaving the British workman to starve at home.

Free-Trade, which has developed free-imports on o ir side only, threatens the commercial ruin of England. Working-men are at last commencing to study this trade question in downright earnest.

This is no longer a party question.

I remain, Sir, a British Elector.

OUR FREE-IMPORTING SYSTEM

ADMITS COMPETING ARTICLES DUTY FREE WHILE BRITISH GOODS ARE TAXED IN EVERY PORT IN THE WORLD.

Open Letter to the Right Hon. Joseph Chamberlain, M.P.

SIR,—I beg to submit the following questions to your notice :—

Do you believe that free-trade—which has settled down to a policy of free-importation—has fulfilled the expectations of its authors, or really benefits the working man?

Is cheap bread a boon to the working classes, when the same policy which admits the surplus wheat stocks of the world also permits the free-importation of cheap goods made by the sweaters of Europe, who work their hands 70 hours a week, and thus robs the British mechanic of his rightful labour, and thrusts him on the streets; to say nothing of our partially ruined agriculture? Is not a cheap loaf a pitiful recompense? or I might pertinently ask, What does the cheap loaf really cost?

Do you believe that our excessive imports benefit the nation; or that our dependence upon foreign countries for the bulk of our food is not a grave peril to the British people?

Are you aware that the years of the greatest prosperity in this generation were in 1871-2-3-4, and that in those four years our exports exceeded our imports by £28,000,000 sterling?

Do you know that under our free-trade system the poor man is taxed more heavily than the rich? as, for instance, out of each shilling spent by the mechanic in cocoa, he pays 1¾d. tax; for each shilling in coffee, 2½d.; raisins, 4d.; currants, 3½d.; tea, 4d.; and tobacco 9¾d.; while the silks, lace, and fancy hosiery bought by the rich are free of tax.

As you must be well acquainted with the extent and undeveloped rescources of the British Empire, do you think that any lasting federation can be achieved on any other basis than that of favoured trade and commercial union?

Do you perceive any successful future for British productive industry unless the markets are fostered within the Empire?

To put a case in point, do you think that the brass and other trades in Birmingham, and other industries in large towns, can for long withstand the free-importation of the products of Continental and American labour, which reach us as surplus from protected markets?

Do you think that anything short of retaliation upon the competing goods of other nations will procure a practical measure of free-trade, that is a free, or nearly free, market for British exports?

Have you carefully weighed the fact that Britain's industrial rivals have, of efficiency in most trades, reached the British standard, and that it has become a question of the relative taxation borne by each international competitor, as to his chance in the commercial race?

Are you aware that our free-trade benefits all the nations abroad, and our profit-mongers at home, and makes foreign nations of our Colonies, while it starves the farm-labourer and stultifies the efforts of the trade-unionist, by keeping thousands of our workers and mechanics on the streets?

Have you observed that this is not a party question, but a people's question, and one that will not wait?

I remain, Sir, a Working-man Elector.

UNITED EMPIRE & BETTER TRADE.

A Reply to the Cobden Club Leaflet, No. 88.

An agitation for the Commercial Federation of the British Empire on practicable lines is afoot, and promises to become a burning question.
The British and Irish working men and manufacturers, finding the home trade relatively contracting, by the inroad of foreign competing goods, and the export market closing upon them by increasingly hostile tariffs, and even their own colonies, planted with such enterprize and zeal by their fore-fathers, slipping away from them, are at last determined to make a bold stand in defence of their own and their children's rights, and preserve the Empire and its splendid resources largely for the use of British and Colonial citizens. To this end they are advocating the policy of preferential treatment of Anglo-Colonial products over those of the foreigner, who unfairly restricts British goods. In other words, to moderately tax the goods of the foreigner in favour of the Colonies, and they by a lighter tax to give British and Irish goods a preference in their markets. This is as it should always have been, unless foreign nations had given us a free-market in return for our open ports.

This discrimination against the goods of the foreigner in favour of our own Colonies, in order to cement the bonds of union on a lasting basis, is calculated to enormously increase our home and external trade, create better employment and more wages, and, in the end, lessen the hours of labour for the British workman.

The Cobden Club (Leaflet No. 88) says " that it is almost impossible to federate the British Empire, because part is on a free-trade basis, and the other portion has a policy of protection.

" That if we did federate, it would make food dear and trade and employment scarce, and rob us of the foreign markets for our goods, and render the foreigner our enemy "

This view of the case is purely imaginary and miserably incorrect. It will not stand the slightest test of practical and analogous investigation So far from there being any difficulty in federating the various parts of the British Empire, each portion, with an official voice of its own, has been waiting for years for the Mother Country to propose a plan for uniting the whole Empire on a trade basis. It must be on a commercial foundation. It is perfectly useless to speak of Imperial Federation on any other policy. It has been open to the Colonies to federate on a sentiment of free-trade ever since they have had existence. But they have refused, and to-day it is hopeless to expect them to alter in this essential respect. The Colonists are business people, and want something in return for something. We must offer to give the wheat, wool, fruit, and other productions of our Colonies a distinct preference—not large, say ten per cent., over the competing imports from foreign nations—the Colonies returning the favour—if any lasting or even possible scheme of unity be attempted.

The recent Australasian Federation Convention, affords a strong proof that the difficulties in the way of commercial unity can speedily be removed.

It requires a policy of give-and-take all round, and then the matter is simple enough.

Such a plan would not destroy our foreign trade. It might, indeed, lessen some of our foreign imports of food and other commodities, and afford us a better chance of raising and making these productions at home or in our own Colonies, and thus provide more employment for our own people.

France, Germany, and Spain, that give preference to their Colonies, do not injure their foreign commerce, while by their wise and far-seeing policy they are building up great dominions behind the seas that will remain permanent partners of their respective parent States.

Sir Joseph Crowe, in his recent Official Report to the British Government and Parliament on the external trade of France since 1860, shows how enormously the French have increased their exports to England between 1881 and 1890; especially in silks and woollen goods, and the large decrease of our exports of goods to the French during the same period. This has thrown vast numbers of British workmen out of employment at their regular trades. Such results would not, however, be so disastrous if the workers thus driven from their own trades could readily find employment at other industries, for which the British people were better adapted. But it is not so. Displaced labour must either emigrate or go to swell the mighty army of the unemployed. England has more honest and willing workers idle than any country in the world

Bread—if England federates with her Colonies—can never become dear again. Steam, telegraphy, and cheap and rapid transit of wheat, will always prevent the price rising much, even with a moderate duty on corn. The nations that tax corn, viz., France, Germany, Austria, Belgium, and America, have the price of bread about the same as ours, while they each and all, or nearly all, pocket a large revenue by the tax on imported wheat.

Look at the national danger we incur in case of war by the policy of importing one-half our food supply, to say nothing of the cost in times of peace in maintaining our extra large Navy to protect our food ships. During a portion of 1890, according to a statement in the House of Commons, there was only seven weeks' stock of wheat in hand in the whole country. Think of this state of things, and the fact that we have driven half-a-million farm labourers from the soil, and millions of acres out of wheat and other cultivation. If we desire to retain our Colonies in close unity with us, and to develop their vast resources, and thus enable them to raise much of our food and raw material, and to grow prosperous and wealthy, that they may materially help to defend our over-sea commerce, we must build up a mighty trading and industrial federation between ourselves and the several parts of our magnificent inheritance. Foreign nations, while they have learned much from us, have taught the British people—by their hostile tariffs, which destroy our export trade, and by their favoured treatment of their own Colonies—the mine of wealth we possess in our vast dominions, the federation of which would make us independent of the whole world.

If we do not wish to see our two greatest Colonies, viz., Canada and Australia, drifting off to commercial union with the United States, and putting on an extra tax on our exported goods in favour of the workers and the traders of that great country, we have not a moment to lose. It is no longer an economic question. It is a game of political and commercial chess. Working men, take up your electoral arms, and fight manfully for your trade and industries, which means your daily bread. The world has entirely changed since we began the free-trade experiment. No nation will trade freely with us. Look upon all who speak in favour of free-imports of foreign competing goods as your worst enemy. That cry is played out. Since we cannot get real free-trade, we must resolve in dead earnest to safeguard all that is left to us, viz., our Colonial Empire. In 1892, France gave her Colonies a fifty per cent preference, and also followed the lead of the United States, and brought into action a McKinley Bill of their own, which will increase the taxes on sections of our exported goods from 20 to 100 per cent.

A child would see the force and the drift of these facts.

The last elections in Canada, and the constantly-recurring agitation for commercial reciprocity between the Dominion and the United States, have shown most conclusively that Great Britain must either favour the chief productions of her Empire, and Canada in particular, or give up Canada and dismember the Empire. We cannot have free-imports and Canada. If ever the British people hope to obtain an " Eight-Hours " Day, it can come only by securing large Home and Colonial Markets for our manufactured goods, and taxing the foreigner, who sweats his workmen by forcing them to labour eleven hours per day.

Lord Playfair, when presiding at the last free-trade banquet, at Greenwich, on July 1st, 1893, said—in the course of a speech that was singularly lacking in an up-to-date grasp of the industrial situation—that we must wait until the Colonies gave the Mother Country free-markets for her exports, before we can arrange an Imperial Commercial Union. This contention is manifestly absurd on the face of it, as it would be almost equivalent to bidding us wait for universal free-trade before we sought Inter-British Commercial Union.

The old Chartists foresaw the result of free-imports, and prophesied that the land would be thrown out of cultivation, the agricultural labourer starved, factories closed, and the artizan driven to the workhouse. Is not this doleful picture of industrial life fully realized in 1893 ? The

American Bill is causing scores of large firms to stop production already, and when the results of the United States treaties (treaties rendered possible by the McKinley Bill) with Brazil and Venezuela are felt, more British export trade will be lost. Our free-imports are responsible for all this damage to the interests of the British producer—the working man No country would dare to block out our goods if they feared reprisals. It is because they think that they can safely count upon blind adherence to the free-trade fetish that they act in this selfish manner.

The Cobden Club contends that we would forfeit the privileges of the "Most Favoured Nation" Clause in our dealings with foreign countries, if we taxed foreign imports to give our Colonies a preference. This reasoning is manifestly absurd Great Britain and her Colonies once federated, they would be looked upon as one great nation, and would be accorded the same advantages which France, Germany, and Spain have always had in the matter of their respective Colonies. The policy of discrimination in favour of our Colonies once adopted, it would be comparatively easy for the British Government to secure the "Most Favoured Nation" treatment, because it would possess the necessary power to enforce it by discriminating against the offending party.

The question of a moderate and a high tariff is as peace is to war.

It should never be forgotten that the commercial federation of the British Empire possesses a moral aspect of overshadowing importance.

Great Britain and her Colonies have been in the vanguard of civilization ; promoting the enduring arts of peace, representative institutions, and the amelioration of the hard condition of the working classes. In the latter category we have the Factory Acts and the reduction of the hours of labour. To remain in this proud position Great Britain must unite in trade, industry, and commerce with her great Colonies. The German and French Empires, and the mighty Republic of the United States, are resolved to shut out the bulk of our exports—the workman's daily bread—by heavy tariffs. How otherwise than by a trade-union with her Colonies can England maintain her commercial supremacy, or continue in the commanding position of guiding the world for peace ? Once having lost her trade, her wealth, her flag and her prestige would be gone, and the mighty Empire that could have been, would become three or four fifth-rate powers, at the mercy of the military forces of Europe. Unity and Consolidation are the modern laws of progress. Let us, therefore, unite. We cannot unite by sentiment alone. Real free-trade, as Cobden defined it, has never existed ; let us, therefore, cease to worship and practice the sham free-trade of free-imports, and offer to our Colonies those solid advantages of favoured trade, which alone will secure an United Empire.

Defend your Colonial markets ; stand by your home trade ; protect your labour ; labour before party, and the British Colonies for the British.

THE AGRICULTURAL CRISIS.

A Word to Agriculturalists, their Labourers, and the Public.

British wheat is taxed about four shillings per quarter, while foreign corn enters the English market free. Is this doing justice to British labour?

The wheat imported into England duty free, comes mainly from America, Russia, and India. It is part of the American *surplus*, which can be sold at *any price*, and the produce of Russia and India, where the poor labourers are compelled to work for *sixpence a day*.

Farm labourers, think of these facts, and ponder over them for yourselves.

It is urged, by arm-chair Economists, that we *must* admit this wheat duty free. The answer to them is simple and effective. Great Britain cannot afford to have her agriculture crushed out of existence by such unjust and unfair competition. Labourers, think of your future and that of your children. Work can no longer be found for you in the towns as in years gone by. The great trades are now in the same plight as agriculture. Thanks to the national folly of free-imports (shamefacedly called free-trade), fully manufactured goods are met with hostile tariffs abroad, and ruinous competition at home. Artisans are, as a consequence, starving in our great cities. The system of sham free-trade suits the rich classes with fixed incomes, but cuts on every side against the real interest of British working men.

It has been calculated that the fall in the value in agricultural produce in 1891, as compared with 1871, reaches the enormous total of £77,000,000 sterling, or an average of £1 12s. 4½d. per acre How can the farm-labourer get proper wages under such conditions as these?

If much of the land in Great Britain was *given rent free*, the farmers could not pay their way and give fair wages to the labourers at present prices, and existing taxation. Part of the tax on the British farmer goes to build ships of war to safeguard foreign-grown food in its transit on the high seas. Why should not the foreigner pay this tax?

The farm-labourers in common with the artisans in the town, must agitate for justice and fair-play for British industries. Party politics cannot aid them. A pull all-together to demand fair conditions for labour is all that is needed.

Cheap bread and no money to buy it means the workhouse for everybody. The British workman was better off when bread was 7d. and even 8d. a loaf, as in the years 1871-2-3-4, because trade was good.

The writers in the press who uphold free-imports should be asked to labour for half-fee.

A four shilling tax on each quarter of foreign wheat would barely equal the taxes borne by the British farmer. Every nation on the face of the earth has a tax on foreign wheat.

President Cleveland, who is said to favour free-trade, is willing to keep a revenue duty of 8s. in the pound on dutiable imports, and 6s 8d. on each quarter of wheat. Where does the free-trade come in?

The cry is, *take the tax off food-raising land*, or place an equal one on the foreign wheat, and thus give the English farmer a chance to make both ends meet, and to pay his labourers living wages. Let the cry go forth, *save British Agriculture!*

OPEN LETTER TO TRADE-UNIONISTS.

WORKING MEN,—It affords me great pleasure to address a few words to you on British industry.

Since you have wisely combined to defend daily labour, it follows as a logical necessity that you are also organized to safeguard British trade; and any power or policy which destroys that trade, prevents you from obtaining the work, the fair rate-of-wages, and the other beneficial results which should be the practical outcome of your union.

As experienced business men, you are well aware that the value of the capital represented by your and the nation's skilled labour, is about equal in amount to the value in plant and currency in the whole country, and that the policy of free-imports which unfairly floods the British markets with foreign-made goods, and thereby deprives you of your labour and forces you upon the streets, must entail widespread distress and grave national loss. There are, it is authoritatively estimated, a million-and-a-half of workers idle at the present time.

As organized workers you well know that your first duty is to protect the producer—not by bolstering up his labour beyond its real economic value, but insisting upon fair conditions. The consumer can take care of himself. The masses are the producers. Good wages for honest work, can afford fair prices for all commodities, which are the productions of others ; but, on the other hand, poor pay and scant work find things dear at almost any low price.

As British producers possessed of common-sense, you may readily perceive that dirt-cheap bread, which ruins our agriculture and starves the farm-labourer, in the same manner as low priced foreign goods—made by the sweaters of Europe—curtail our town trade, cannot be really cheap, since it robs you of your rightful labour and its just rewards.

Since the year 1846—when the British Government adopted the policy of free-imports, with the hope of converting other countries to this economic system—the great nations have one and all become manufacturing rivals, and with one sweet accord *have closed their ports with tariffs to British goods*, so far as profitable trade is concerned. They have taken our mechanical inventions, but with one voice scornfully reject our free-trade. We are, therefore, left with open ports, defenceless against the surplus prices, the long hours of Europe, and the over-production of the whole world, while our vast Colonies and dependencies—which might raise all our imported raw material, and much of our food, and take our manufactured goods in exchange—are, by our policy of free-imports, treated as foreign countries.

As the markets abroad are closing to us, where shall we find future trade outlets, if not in our own Empire ? Is it not, therefore, time to demand that favoured trade terms be made with our Colonies and Possessions ?

The organized workers in the country—the majority of the electors—have this matter largely in their own hands. With you rest the power to stop the free and untaxed importation of sixty-five millions sterling per annum of manufactured goods, and one hundred and fifty millions sterling of food—much of which should be raised at home. British industry bears the whole cost of national government, and yet the foreigner finds here a free-market for his over-production, without a single sixpence for toll.

Our naval power (mainly supported by the British workman) our wealth and our prestige maintain the independence of our Empire, and there, also, we provide a ready-made market for the entire world on the same terms as to ourselves, and to the shameful neglect of British and Colonial trade.

In the prosperous years 1871-2-3-4, we cheerfully paid a good price for food, and agriculture flourished.

A Trade-Union of Commerce with our Colonies and the entire Empire, is an economic and fiscal necessity of the time, and the best step to ensure the industrial and social welfare of the various sections of workers concerned.

SHAM FREE-TRADE :

THE RUIN OF BRITISH LABOUR.

An Address to Working Men.

We live by labour, and that which robs us of our trade, takes the bread from our mouths and keeps us in misery ! The national policy which lets in cheap-made foreign goods and wheat, *duty free,* must take our work away and help to lower our wages.

Of what use, therefore, are cheap articles from abroad, if they do not make us better off ? And how can they do that if they cause our trade to fall off ? This applies just as much to foreign wheat and flour as it does to general goods. If farm-labourers are out of work it affects us in the large towns—we sell less. Other nations refuse to have our goods without we pay a heavy tax : and yet you hear some foolish persons talk about our having *free-trade.* The present system suits some factors and merchants, who buy these cheap foreign goods, and sell them here, while we often starve for the want of work.

The foolish, or knavish free-trader, tells us that free-trade gives us cheap food. What we want to know is, does it give us plenty of *work* and *good wages* ? That is the point, that is the question to deal with. The first thing and the last thing to consider is, how to get plenty of profitable trade. We let goods in free, and find the foreigner the trade, and go without ourselves.

Fellow working men, let us call upon free-traders to prove the benefits of what they call free-trade. We have believed them long enough Now, we ask for proof that our falsely called free-trade, is anything else than a striking injustice to British labour. It matters not, whether a man calls himself a trade-unionist, a labour advocate, a Liberal, or a Socialist, if he upholds the present ruinous system, he is an enemy to the working man and the country's progress, and should be called upon to give reliable evidence in support of his position, or frankly admit his own ignorance on the question. As a matter of fact, all those who uphold the English system of *sham free-trade* are ignorant of the real nature of this serious trade question, and should be told so.

The matter is very simple—we let foreign goods in free, but no nation will give us the same advantage, they tax our goods and shut us out, while they pour more and more of their stuff in our markets, and thus steal our home trade.

Sham free-traders have no logical argument, no real facts in support of their position, they have instead, simply a blind belief in its favour. What a specimen of political wisdom! They make free-trade a party question, which is another proof of their folly.

Working men! Ask sham free-traders where the future markets for British and Irish goods are? They cannot tell you. The good-trader knows and can show the way to get them. We have great Colonies—Canada, Australia, etc.—which would give us unlimited markets for our hardware, jewellery, pottery, cotton and woollen goods, if we would tax the foreigner and give them—our Colonists—a free or nearly free market for their produce: wheat, fruit, meat, etc

Working men, we must stand no more nonsense about what is falsely called free-trade, we must resolve to fight down the ruinous idea. Our Parliamentary Representatives must pledge themselves to abolish free-imports, and thus give us the control of our own trade, both at home and in our Colonies. Be not deceived with the cry about taxing wheat and making bread dear. Bread can never be dear again if we tax foreign wheat, and grow more of it at home and in our own Colonies. Under the present system, however, of feeding the people with foreign corn, we might be starved to death if a war caused the supply to be cut off.

Working men in the towns, think of the poor and sweated farm-labourer in the country, who has been robbed of his work, and deprived of good wages, by the free-importation of foreign wheat: and the same policy also takes your own trade away, by letting in cheap foreign goods. Of what use then, is dirt-cheap bread, if the free-import system which gives it you, also lowers your wages and destroys your trade ?

The prosperity and commercial future of the British race are assured, if British labour be properly defended by taxing foreign goods, and giving favoured trade terms to our Colonies.

Now the points to be remembered are these:

1st. The sham free-trade robs you of your trade, by letting in cheap foreign goods duty free, and without paying a penny tax for the use of our markets. Real free-trade is wanted, and no other will do.

2nd. That sham free-trade encourages foreign nations to shut out our goods by heavy taxes, since they have nothing to fear from retaliation. They secure their own home markets, and have the free use of ours as well.

3rd. That sham free-trade prevents us making the best trade arrangements with our Colonies, as it leaves us nothing to offer or bargain with. For instance, if they—our Colonies—desired to give our goods the preference before those of foreigners, we have no advantages to give our Colonies in return, as we let foreign goods in duty free.

4th. That free-trade does not exist, as no nation will trade freely with us, we have simply the free-importation of foreign goods, which is injurious to British and Irish labour. Sixty-five millions sterling of manufactured goods came in free last year, to compete with us.

5th. That the countries that will not adopt free imports progress faster than we do. Five hundred millions of civilized people refuse free-trade. England stands alone.

6th. That sham free-trade has been made a party cry by the Liberals, which is a serious evil, as it leads working men to think that our free-trade (which is not free-trade at all) must be good for the people, whereas it is the *greatest curse*.

7th. That the question of real free-trade, instead of sham free-trade, is a national question, a working man's question, and the cry should be, *abolish free-imports, and defend British labour!*

BRITISH FREE-TRADE.

A Dialogue between two Working Men.

GEORGE *(who believes in free-trade)* : Hallo, Tom ! is it true that you are doing *no work* lately ?

TOM *(who has seen the bad effects of free-imports)* : Yes. Since that last ship-load of *cheap foreign goods* came in, we've been shut at our place.

GEORGE : Well, I suppose that the foreigners can make them *cheaper* than you can ; so you see it can't be helped. It's *right* for everybody to buy in the *cheapest* market, isn't it ?

TOM : Yes, when the conditions are fair and equal. We should not think it *right* for our employer to set on a man in our place simply because he would work for five shillings *less wages*. He might be a single man, or a foreigner who lives on a bit of fruit. In the same way, I think that the cheap foreign goods that come in *duty free*, and cuts us out, while they *tax* our English articles in their markets, is trading in an unfair way. Let 'em pay the taxes to keep this country going as we do, and then they won't undersell us much I guess.

GEORGE : Isn't there *other reasons* why they make goods so cheap, besides having none of our taxes to pay ?

Tom : Yes, you're right, there are. They work *longer* hours and get *less* wages than we do.

George: Now, Tom. I think that you have *condemned* yourself. You want to make me believe that these foreigners have a *better plan* of doing trade than we have, and yet you admit that they are *forced* to work longer hours and for less wages than we do

Tom : That *puzzled* me a bit at first, but after reading a little about it, I soon saw how it was. You see, George, these foreign countries have been manufacturing on a large scale with steam machinery for a few years only. The free-traders, or, as I prefer to call them, the free-importers, in those early free-importing days, thought that foreigners would never be able to manufacture like us, but have to grow food and raise raw materials for our market. The foreigners are not yet so quick and expert in many things as we are—for we had a long start you know, and it takes them longer to turn out the stuff. But if you will go back forty years, and see what their hours and wages were to what they are now, you will find that they have got on *faster* than we have. If you really want a good test of the practical effects of a policy of rightly defending home labour, you must look to America, where wages in most trades are *half as much again* as ours, and most things as cheap, some cheaper than in England.

George : The great thing is, that free-trade gives us *cheap bread.*

TOM : I see, GEORGE, that you have been caught by that *clap-trap*, as I was once. Cheap bread isn't everything. Plenty of work at good wages is the first matter to think about. Dirt-cheap bread is *dear* to every working man. We let in the wheat-sweepings of the world *duty free*, and ruin our farmers and their labourers, just the same as the bringing in of cheap foreign goods ruin us in the towns. Besides, you must know, that the farmers and their men in the country, when they have money, are our *best* customers for the articles we make in our shops and factories. Bread will *never* be dear again, not even with a *tax* upon it, to give our farmers fair-play. Bread was dearest when there was no tax on it.

GEORGE : I must say that I never saw things in that light before

TOM : You know Jack Wilson, George? Well, he's been in regular work for a long time at his place. They make goods for the Cape Colonies and Canada, and I have been told that they are our *best* customers, and if we were to moderately tax the stuff from foreign nations, and let in wheat, meat, fruit and all other things from our Colonies *free*, or nearly free, it would bring us two or three times the trade, as they— our Colonies—would have *more* goods from us in return. There needs a little manœuvring in this matter, George, don't you see?

GEORGE : I never heard free-trade argued in that way. It seems to me that things have *altered* in other countries since we took to it.

Tom : The fact is, we thought because it was the Liberals that advocated free-trade, that it must be for the benefit of the people. So it would if foreigners would let us enter their markets, but they won't. I can see now that it is nothing to do with *party-politics*. Any Government can get us fair-play in trade if we send members to Parliament pledged to demand it. We are the *only nation* on the face of the earth which keeps open markets for everybody. Let us form a trades-union with our vast Colonies. We would be *independent* of the foreign markets, and we would then have *more real free-trade* than Cobden and Bright dreamt about, and by that means bring the foreigners to their knees, and get fair dealings from them.

George : It always puzzled me why so many of our best mechanics went to America. I begin to see it now. The Americans take care that they are not unfairly dealt with by the *free* admission of goods made by next-door to pauper labour. It seems like a labour and a trades-union question when it is looked at closely.

Tom : Your reference to America just reminds me that Bill Simmons has been thrown out from his place ever since the Americans passed that McKinley Act. You see this is another way our free-importing system works, it allows the foreigners to tax our exports how they like, and turn us who make the goods on the streets.

Good morning George, I see that you are beginning to think for yourself, and find that the *free*-importation of competing foreign goods is a *labour* question, and touches work and wages in a direct manner. Keep your eye on it, and don't be mislead by Liberal oratory or newspaper fudge—they have no cheap American or German editions to compete with.

GEORGE : Good bye, Tom. I shall think more about this matter in future. As you say, cheap bread (which has been brought down in price perhaps by sweating) isn't everything.

THE CHIEF OPPONENTS OF SHORTER HOURS OF LABOUR.

An Open Letter to the British Advocates of an Eight Hours' Day.

The shortening of the hours of labour is, without question, one of the most important reforms for the uplifting of the masses, and the true advancement of the nation, that has ever found advocacy; because, in the nature of things, the liberation of the body from the thrall of excessive physical exertion, means the freedom of the mind to attain that higher and better form of government, which is the constant aim and desire of mankind. To this extent, I am in hearty and sincere agreement with your aims.

Great Britain has an honourable record in the movement for the reduction of the hours of labour. Robert Owen, and a host of earnest Reformers, gave an early start to this civilizing power, the effects of which have helped to raise the intelligence, and the standard of living in the nation at large. The British people, at the present time, labour for less hours than those of any other great industrial power—thanks to labour organization and popular leaders.

The social and moral good which result from the lessening of the hours of labour, is, fortunately in our day, a matter removed from the sphere of controversy. But the moment the question of a further reduction in the length of daily toil is looked at from economic and industrial points of view, the difficulties commence. In a country like Great Britain, which has developed a foreign trade in manufactures of somewhat abnormal demensions, and increasingly hard to maintain, on account of the rapid progress of her industrial rivals, the question of lessening the hours of labour, and probably increasing the cost of production, is one of very grave importance. The willingness of some sections of workers to take a corresponding reduction in wages for the shorter hours, could not be applied to the whole body of toilers, as there are vast numbers who could not take less weekly pay. Even on the supposition that the reduction in wages could be generally enforced, it would not be an improvement to the masses. If ten millions of workers, who laboured nine hours per day, were willing to take a strictly reduced wage for an eight-hours day, and another million and a quarter toilers were placed in employment to fill up the deficiency of ten millions of hours—caused by such time reform—and received the portion of the wage voluntarily surrendered by the ten millions, as their pay, in what way would this improve matters? The same amount of wages, formerly earned by the ten millions, would be spread over the eleven millions and a quarter. The spending power of the larger number of workers would but just equal the outgoings of the smaller body.

That is a state of things extremely unsatisfactory, and not to be tolerated. A reduction in the hours of labour should synchronize with a *rise, not with a fall* in wages, since the wants of the workers would increase with the curtailment of toil. I am, therefore, much opposed to those among you who look upon the shortening of the hours of labour chiefly as a means to provide work for the unemployed, because such an equalisation alone would greatly tend to drag down the whole mass of workers to a lower level. That such views should be held by considerable numbers of the working classes, serves to show the slender knowledge which exists, concerning the basis of British industry, and its international environment. The labour leaders —who should be well grounded in a knowledge of the external and internal economic conditions which surround British industry—are, I regret to state, very inadequately informed concerning the fiscal isolation of Great Britain, and the consequent helplessness of English producers to mould and fashion their industrial destiny. The power to direct the commercial current of British industrialism, has passed from the labour captains of England, to the foreign tariff-framers, and the exploiters of the lower labour levels of the world. British industry, is in the position of a dismantled ship floating on the open sea of commerce, and at the mercy of every tariff-current, and low-priced labour winds which may assail her from any quarter of the globe. It is useless for old fashioned and out-of-date reasoners to doubt this statement. It is writ large on every page of our commercial history since 1875. In the latter year, the British nation entered upon its career of free-imports for all competing goods, having taken off the last five-and-a-half millions sterling of customs duties in 1871-2-3 and 4. From that date, we ceased to possess any practical control over the productive industries of the nation, whether for home, or foreign exchange. *The chief opponents, therefore, of the " eight-hours day " are the supporters of Britain's crude, and politically-criminal policy of free-imports on the one hand, and the foreign protectionists on the other.* Bricks cannot be made without clay, and the hours of labour cannot be reduced, while a million-and-a-half of unemployed workers press like a hungry army on the heels of the engaged toilers. Paradoxical as it may appear, it is nevertheless a sound economic truth, that the hours of labour can be shortened only when all workers are profitably employed. When ten per cent. of the working army are forced out of the industrial ranks, it points, not to a reduction of the daily term of employment of the active majority, but rather to the *increase* of the working hours, or a drop in the rate of pay.

As I am a staunch opponent of either the lengthening of working hours, or the lowering of wages, I address this letter to you in the hope, that you may seriously consider the present fiscal policy of Great Britain, and its special bearing upon the eight-hours question at the present juncture.

If it be true that the nation cannot reduce the hours of its workers when trade depression exists, and a vast number of hands are idle, it is of the highest importance that an enquiry be made into the cause of the industrial stagnation, with a view to its prompt removal, and the production of a state of things which would admit of "Time Reform." British production is abnormally depressed at the present time. High tariffs abroad, and free-imports of competing goods at home, operate to the artificial restriction of English production. To increase demand for British products, manufacturers and producers on every side are calling out for a reduction in wages. This proves the truth of my statement, that hours of labour can be shortened only in times of industrial activity. Periods of depression, suggest the contrary process, or the lowering of pay.

National production is artificially curtailed. British productions have to compete abroad with goods made in protected markets, and with foreign commodities admitted duty free, at home, while a heavy burden of local and Imperial taxation handicaps them in the place of origin, and heavy duties meet them when exported, from which their foreign rivals are almost free.

When the "Ten Hours Movement" was won, and the "Nine-Hours Day" achieved, British industry was not in its present plight. Our industrial competitors had not developed their productive abilities, and the British people had not abandoned their power to make advantageous commercial treaties, and to prevent high tariffs being enforced against them.*

It is probable, that at this point, I shall be reminded that the great industrial nations who have retained their tariffs on competing imports are worse off than ourselves in the matter of hours of labour, since France and Germany have a working day of eleven hours, and

---

* The writer maintained this position in London, in 1891, during a public discussion on "Free-Imports and an Eight-Hours Day" with Professor Sydney Webb, L L.B., L.C.C., Lecturer on Political Economy at the London University.

the United States of America one of ten hours. The cause of this does not appear on the surface. It is, however, susceptible of easy demonstration that their onger hours of labour are not traceable to their tariffs, although the latter are unreasonably heavy and restrictive. Substantial tariffs in our own case did not prevent our obtaining first a ten, and afterwards a nine-hours day. It is clear, therefore, that tariffs, do not of themselves, either prevent or secure the reduction in the daily toil of a nation. Industrial prosperity, and enlightened labour organization, are the conditions above all others, which render time-reform possible. In the case of France and Germany, their increasing productive activity has synchronized with our advancing industrial depression, and it only needed the freedom, and the aptitude of the British worker for labour organization, on the part of the French and German workers, to secure for them as large a measure of progress, in the way of reduction in their hours of labour, as their British co-workers have achieved. It is also well-known that compulsory military service is a great hindrance to the shortening of hours of labour on the continent of Europe. The case of the hours of labour in the United States of America is a very different one. I have had two years' valuable experience in the American labour field, and I can state most positively, that nothing stood in the way of a general eight-hours day throughout the manufacturing States, but the enormous inrush of what the Americans describe as the "pauper labour" of Europe. Now, that the indiscriminate reception of the surplus population of the world has been stopped, an early inauguration of a general eight-hours day, may be confidently expected. The conditions of productive activity and labour organization, which I regard as basic, and bed-rock needs in this matter, are fairly-well supplied in the United States.

In our own case, one of the conditions, viz., the organization of labour, was never before so promising. But, unfortunately, British production is, relatively, at an exceedingly low ebb. Every staple industry, is in an apparently chronic state of partial collapse. Thousands of workers in each branch are forced into idleness. The present position, and future prospects of the vast army of colliers, is grave in the extreme. A four-hours day would be needed to keep the colliers employed in the existing condition of British industry. This would mean a double labour bill, and coal at famine prices. These would re-act disastrously upon each and all other branches of labour. No, nothing can be attempted in the hours-reform movement, until British labour interests are placed upon a sound economic and fiscal basis, and English commerce brought up to a normal level of progressive prosperity.

You must, I think, in common justice, admit that the present fiscal basis of British production is grossly unjust, and absurdly unfair. British production is almost exclusively burdened with the Imperial and local taxation of the country: a crushing weight, which amounts to the enormous total of 142 millions sterling. In addition to this, British products contribute to the national taxation of other countries by paying heavy customs duties on entering foreign ports.

I respectfully urge upon you the necessity for the abolition of free-imports, and the inauguration of the much-needed policy of free-exchange, between Great Britain and her world-wide trading partners, or failing this, the equalization of the taxation between all producers, whether native or foreign. Such assimilation in the international incidence of taxation, in connection with exchangable commodities, is of the essence of free-trade, and therefore, eminently desirable. If England is to retain her Empire, and her position in the scale of nations, she must speedily restore the only condition that is needed, to enable her to liberate, for thoughtful leisure, one of the working hours of the toiling masses. That condition is productive activity, and the latter can be brought about by the enforcement of strictly sound fiscal modes in disposing of British products, alike in the home, as in the foreign markets. Equal taxation, and exchangable free-trade for the products of British labour. Prosperous trade would follow, and, as a corollary, an "eight-hours" day.

WHEN IS FOOD CHEAP?

It is the pivotal contention of those who support the policy of free-imports, that the system renders possible a constant supply of cheap food. This is true only in a minor degree. Tariffs of themselves—unless prohibitive in height, in a country that habitually raises but little food—are almost powerless to force prices up, and as a logical corollary, it follows that the abolition of customs dues on food imports, cannot by its inviting influence alone, make food cheap. To make this position impregnable, it is necessary only to state a few present-day facts, and make one or two historical references. In the present year food is cheap in all civilised parts of the globe. Why is food at low prices throughout the world? Is it because the Statesmen of foreign countries have at last been converted to the British policy of free-imports? It might very reasonably be inferred from many of the trumpet-tongued assertions of pseudo-economists at home, that food could not be low-priced, unless by virtue of the miracle-working power of free-imports. Yet, in every country in the world, the price of food rules low, and that in despite of heavy tariffs, and in many instances, the need of importing largely. What is the cause of this economic phenomenon? A too abundant world's supply. Let this diminish to the smallest degree below the average normal needs of the world's population, and the price of food, would rise with the same certainty as the water of a river after rain. The absence of tariffs would not affect the matter. As the policy of free-imports cannot claim the paternity of cheapness, it must not, in common economic justice, be charged with causing a rise in prices. If it could, the indictment would be a strong one indeed. Notice one or two historical facts concerning prices of bread, and it will be at once apparent how small a part the policy of free-imports has played in the trend of food values during the present century. In 1812, the price of a four-pound loaf was one shilling and nine pence ; in 1856, eleven pence half-penny ; and in 1874, eight pence half-penny. The average price of wheat for these particular years were one-hundred-and-twenty-six shillings and six-pence, in the first period ; seventy-three shillings and a penny, in the second ; and fifty-nine shillings and twopence, in the third. In the first and third periods, wheat was admitted duty free, and in the second, the nominal duty of one shilling per quarter was exacted, merely as a registration fee.

It will be pointed out at once that war, with its devastating and decimating powers, was the cause of the scant supply and consequent high prices during the periods named. This does not help the cause of free-imports in the least. It matters not what the nature of the cause of the scarcity may be, it is the fact that a scarcity of itself, be the cause whatever it may, is sufficient to cause a rise in prices, that has to be dealt with. The high price of hay at the present time is distinctly traceable to a scarcity in the hay crop.

Some Economists have tried to prove that the appreciation or depreciation of gold is a ruling cause in the fall or rise in prices. This is, in a sense, equivalent to the statement that, it is not the summer's drought and winter's rain that causes the rise and fall in the water in a river, but the banks on either side which register the rise and fall. As an illustration, the flooding of the river in winter, and its vapourization in summer, with its sequential rise and fall, resembles very closely the fluctuation in prices. The banks bounding the water, guage its level, and gold, registers the price levels of commodities. To reduce the gold appreciation theory to the *reductio-ad-absurdum* point of view, a reference to the price of wheat and of hay will suffice. The latter is dear, while the former is ruinously cheap. Is the dearness of the hay attributable to the depreciation of gold. and the cheapness of wheat to its appreciation? Clearly, the scarcity of the one commodity, and the abundance of the other, is the true and only cause of their relative cheapness, and the reverse. The depreciation of gold in relation to hay, and its appreciation in regard to wheat, are effects not causes. It is not, however, with the cause of cheapness so much as a critical examination of the nature of cheapness, that this section has to pronounce upon. Cheapness, is a relative term. Commodities may be at a low price, and yet be relatively dear if measured by the means of purchasing the same. It has been stated that a bullock may be purchased for twenty shillings, and a four-pound loaf for twopence, in many parts of Asiatic Russia. No one, having to earn a subsistence in those regions, would consider those commodities very cheap. Gauged by the sum for which they would be compelled to sell the products of their own labour, the commodities in question would probably be dear.

To what extent, if any, is food really cheap to the British people ? The displacement of labour, and the consequent loss by want of employment, must be taken into strict account in deciding how far low-priced food may be cheap, and to what extent the people are benefitted or injured by the free-importation of food. The guage of cheapness should be fixed by the average earnings of the masses, and the total number of unemployed—whose displacement from their labour may be traced to the policy of free-imports—as it affects home and export trade. The unemployed must be fed, and the cost, especially when the number is large, reduces in a serious degree, the amount which the employed workers have for their own use and that of their families It low-priced food, imported duty free, tends to throw out of employment large numbers of farm labourers, and causes the demon of insolvency to overtake the farmer, where is the advantage of so-called cheap food ? Is not the food dear at the price ? Should we not place the loss to the unemployed, which the nation at large must indirectly bear, upon the price of the food, to get at its real value ? It is thought by some, that the loss to the country by the low price of food, is a gain to the towns. This assumption, based upon the trade and production of exceptional periods in British commercial history, cannot be sustained by the British, and the world's industrial experience during the last ten years. The free-importation of food injures the workers in the towns as much as the toilers in the country. This statement requires strong argument and adequate proof in its support. And as it has a direct bearing on the question of the relative dearness or cheapness of food, it is most worthy of full consideration.

Cheap commodities, with a fair duty on competing imports, which lighten the burden of internal taxation, is a widely different matter, to one of low-priced commodities and free-ports, with the whole taxation on the home producer. It resolves itself, in its essentials, into a question of relative taxation on production, and the chances, or otherwise, of doing reciprocal trade with those who use British markets.

It has been already stated, that tariffs— unless under very exceptional circumstances— cannot make food dear,* nor does the policy of free-imports possess the power to render food

---

* As a proof in support of this statement, the fact may be cited that wheat was quoted in France, a few years ago, at precisely the same price as that in England, although the former country enforced tariff on imported wheat to the amount of six shillings per quarter.

cheap. The same price for a given weight or measure of food in two countries, both food-importers—the one with free-ports, and the other with a tariff—would, civilization being equal, yield the cheapest food supply to the nation which maintained a light customs duty on its food imports. The reason for this seeming economic paradox, arises from the fact that, the food consumers in the tariff country obtain their food for the same price as those in the free-importing nation, and have in addition the revenue derived from the customs dues on their food imports. The income from the latter source, enables their government, to ease the burden of internal taxation on the home production of the tariff country. Production is thus given an advantage, and is much more likely to pay in times of low prices, than in the free-importing nation.

Admitting that free-imports alone, do not make food cheap, it is clearly manifest that it renders the home production of food relatively dear, by placing the whole weight of national taxation on the native food raiser. To show the true bearing of this side of the case, an estimate of the practical remission of taxation by Great Britain on behalf of her external food suppliers, is instructive. Great Britain imports food annually to the value of one-hundred-and-fifty millions sterling. If these imports were subjected to the same taxation as the British food producers bear, viz., fifteen per cent. of the value, the enormous sum of twenty-two-and-a-half millions sterling would be gathered in for the national exchequer. With so large a revenue from food imports, paid for the use of the British market, much could be done to encourage native agriculture. The taxation on the British food grower might be very greatly reduced, to the direct advantage of the country at large. Nothing tends so materially to make food really cheap, as the full cultivation of the land at home. The land profitably tilled, and the whole body of farm-labourers employed, is the surest means to produce cheap food. Cheapness, is not synonymous with ruinously low prices. The nation that imports a large mass of its food, at prices below which it is able to profitably compete, is paying a dear price for its external supply. The logic of the matter, points to a not distant future, when food would cease to be raised at home, and an absolute and perilous dependence on foreign sources, forced upon the people. It is, in the nature of things, almost impossible to reach such a condition—because the funds with which to purchase such external supplies could not be earned—but an approximation, to economic environments so disastrous, measurably ruins a country, by dislocating its industry and depriving the citizens of their labour.

As the cheapness of food can be tested only by the profitable employment of the masses, it is necessary to trace the influence of the free-importation of food on the export trade of the country The free and indiscriminate importation of food, leaves Great Britain without a single fiscal weapon of defence, or offence, with which to combat the tariff attacks of foreign competitors. The war of tariffs has been continuous and deadly since 1879, and the producers of British exports have had to pay dearly for their entry into the world's markets. The proofs of this are too abundant and conclusive to need further remark The unprofitable nature, and partial collapse, of every staple trade stand as living witnesses of the devastating effects of the fiscal war. Of what use is low-priced food to men who have been deprived of the only means within their power of purchasing anything ? It is worse than useless to refer to cheap food, when the price paid for the same is the nominal price, plus the loss of trade and labour Free-imports is credited with supplying the people with cheap food, but while that assumption may be doubted, it is indisputable that the system supplies *poor people* for cheap food. The poor people, unhappily, exist in hundreds of thousands ; but where is the cheap food ? Low-priced food is undoubtedly cheap to persons with fixed incomes, but to large sections of the workers who vainly seek employment, it is comparatively dear. It may be asked, is it not better to have food at nominally low prices to partly meet the needs of the poor and the unemployed, than to mock them with prohibitive rates ? Yes, if high prices for food and a long-continued national want of employment were possible. High rates for food and a vast army of unemployed never synchronise for long periods. Labour would drift to the land,

and the profits from agriculture, would be spent in the purchase of commodities which would re-act beneficially on all other sections of industry.

The facts that stand most in need of enforcement are, that the policy of free imports, leaves the agriculturalist, in a period of low prices, with the crushing burden of taxation from which his foreign competitor is free. He is thus driven to put his land down to grass, and turn his labourers from their employment. The value of their labour must be placed on the food. They cannot find employment in the towns, because the same fiscal policy which has injured the farmer has in turn re-acted upon the manufacturing industry. The food exporters, having no retaliation from Great Britain to fear, raised their tariffs against British exports and destroyed profitable trade, and robbed the British worker of his labour. Thus it appears, that the self-same system, which is said to give the people cheap food, at one stroke cuts off the trade which is needed to enable the masses to purchase the food. Again, it is necessary to enquire, is this low-priced food cheap?

While it is practically out of the power of any Government to prevent prices of food ruling low, it is well within their province to relieve the home food grower from unjust and exceptional taxation. Again, it is but simple justice to the people that such commodities as tea, coffee, cocoa, currants, raisins, etc., which cannot be grown at home, should be relieved of taxation, and sold at their real value.

A glance at the price of wheat, and the rate of wages, during the last four hundred years, will not be without interest :—

		Per Quarter.		Average weekly wages of Artisans.	
		s.	d.	s.	d.
Price of wheat in	1495	4	0¾ …	3	0
,,	1533	7	8 …	4	0
,,	1563	19	9¾ …	4	6
,,	1593	18	4½ …	4	6
,,	1597	56	10½ …	6	0
,,	1610	40	4 …		
,,	1654	51	4 …	8	6
,,	1661	70	6 …	8	6
,,	1785	43	1 …	10	0
,,	1812	126	6 …	12	0
,,	1846	54	1 …	24	0
,,	1854	72	10 …	24	0
,,	1855	71	10 …	24	0
,,	1856	73	1 …	24	0
,,	1857	59	2 …	24	0
,,	1870	45	11 …	28	0
,,	1871	55	1 …	28	0
,,	1872	56	9 …	30	0
,,	1873	57	8 …	33	0
,,	1874	59	2 …	33	0
,,	1890	31	9 …	30	0
,,	1893	25	0 …	28	0

The figures from 1495 to 1661 are taken from the work, "Six Centuries of Work and Wages," by the late Mr. T. Rogers.

To ascertain the cost of food at the periods when prices for wheat ruled high, it would be necessary to take into account the contemporary rates for meat, milk, butter, fruit and vegetables. These latter were often very low in price, when wheat was high through war, depopulating the villages.

It may with truth be stated, that food in a country is cheap, when moderate prices synchronise with the full employment of all sections of the nation's workers. While very low rates point to semi-barbarism, moderate rates denote a people's progress.

Reform, or Industrial Revolution. Which?

A SOLEMN WARNING TO BRITISH STATESMEN.

It is in no strict sense an usurpation of the privileges and powers of the prophetic vein, to assume that the distant reverberations of the tumult of insipient industrial revolution, may be distinctly heard by the mind's attentive ear. The signs are ominous, and loom large on every side. The ear of the mind, like the eye, may sense the nearness of coming events. Reform, or industrial revolution, is inevitable. In any case, the former is certain of achievement. No nation ever permits the approach of industrial extinction without making strenuous endeavours to avert such calamity. The danger lies in the inability to realise the gravity of the situation in time, and in a period of potential remedial strength. Evidence all too palpably exists, that Great Britain has not sensed the commercial peril in which she is placed, or rightly informed herself of the measure of her industrial decadence. Thousands of patriotic citizens have long known the danger which threatens, and have raised their voices, like men crying in the wilderness. But no responsible Statesman has paid sufficient self-sacrificing heed to the lone prophetic warning. A self-immolating stand, by one or two prominent political leaders, who resolutely refused to move in the nation's affairs, until the voice of economic and fiscal reason was heard in the legislative chamber, would, in all probability, have compelled the single eye of the people to examine the sluice through which the wealth and the productive energy of the country is passing with ever-widening power. But this great and heroic course, has not yet achieved a place in our politico-industrial history. Perhaps it may not be necessary in the future, as a daily-increasing suffering is rapidly educating the masses of the people on the main points of the British trade policy. A leader would not, at the present time, necessarily incur the penalty of official extinction, by making a bold and determined stand in defence of fiscal reform.

Reform, or industrial revolution. The latter word has an ugly sound to British ears, and its employment usually creates a smile expressive of stolid incredulity and indifference. No one appears quite capable of realising, even in thought, the possibility of revolution in these Isles. In a socially-developed and law-abiding country like Great Britain, revolution to be possible—not to say probable—would need a vast and widely-distributed mass of the people in its favour. It is impossible to even imagine such a condition of mind among large numbers of the population in the crowded centres, unless a decisive majority of the nation were socially depressed, hungry, and hopeless. The loss of hope, could fall upon a people only when the last lingering faith and trust in their Parliamentary Representatives, had died out. It is, therefore, clearly manifest to the average reasoner, that only in the event of vast numbers of unemployed—who have become socially degraded, hungry, and hopeless, and politically leaderless—that revolution may unfold its menacing standard.

Between the averaging reasoner and the average observer, there is, at this point, a parting of ways. The former clearly perceives the social, industrial, and political conditions which would render revolution possible, but the latter fails to recognise the rapidly grouping realisation of such conditions. The reasoner has the unfailing logic of principles and historical precedents for his guide, while the poor ordinary observer must perforce rely upon his limited powers of daily observation. The aggregate industrial experience of the British producers during the last few years, would supply the reasoner with such alarm-sounding data. that the words—coming revolution—would force themselves into his conscientiousness, like unwelcome guests.

Party-Government has become so machine-like, in its ironclad programmes, that the people are powerless to move their political leaders until they approach the verge of insurrection, or political revolt. One party in the State is wedded to the cry of free-trade, and although free-trade does not exist—no free-selling for British goods, not even in English markets—

the plank of free-trade, is still maintained, as a vital thing, in its programme. The other party, either because they themselves partly believe in the policy of free-imports, or are afraid to risk their chances of success at a general election— by exposing the sham of the free-trade system— make no sign, and thus the people are left untaught, and without guides, in sullenness, hunger, and discontent, to solve the matter for themselves. The solution from this source points unerringly to industrial revolution. The people will not be driven back in the path of social and industrial progress by frequent reductions in wages. Every retrograde step will be, and must be fiercely contested. What justification exists for the levelling down of British wages to the lowest Continental and Indian basis ? None whatever. The soulless profit-mongers, who deal in the sweated labour productions of India and Europe, alone make this audacious demand.

Reform must be enforced. But what reform ? The reform of the destructive, and labour-crushing policy of free-imports. A commercial system which displaces vast sections of labour, without the incidence of profitable exchange employment, breeds industrial revolution. The policy of free-imports displaces whole branches of labour, without the incidence of sufficient alternative profitable occupations. Hence, the system of free-imports, breeds industrial revolution. The evidence, and the facts in detail, in support of this matter, have been given in other places. But to bring the matter home to a convincing degree, it is necessary to cite striking items of evidence in relation to the subject, and to show the direct bearing of the facts adduced, as proving on which side the balance of such evidence lies.

If it can be shown that the policy of free-imports displaces labour, and dislocates industry, and that such disbanded industries thrust their thousands of workers on the streets to starve and riot, then the policy, can in all fairness be charged with the national loss incidental to such industrial stagnation ; and it may further be saddled with the moral responsibility of the riot and suffering which is an invariable result of each suspension of productive activity. What are the great facts in connection with British productive enterprise during the last three years ? Seven great strikes, with the almost inseparable evils of riot, hunger, misery, and all-engulfing social distress. The great London Docks' Strike led off, and was quickly followed by the Bradford, Durham, South Wales, Lancashire, Hull, and the national coal strike of the present year. Each and all of these strikes are clearly traceable, chiefly to the labour-destroying effects of free-imports. The London Docks' Strike could not have taken place, if it had not been for the fact that tens of thousands of workers had been driven from the British soil, and from other industries, by the inability of English producers to raise food at a profit, or to dispose of sufficient quantites of manufactured goods without loss, either at home or abroad.

Free-imports give a preference for foreign food and goods, by yielding untaxed markets for the reception and encouragement of the same, while the fiscal defencelessness of the policy permitted, if it did actually suggest, the imposition of hostile tariffs on British exports. In either case, British labour suffers. Forced from their native industry, large numbers of the workers found their way to the London Docks, swelling the half-famished, and pity-inspiring crowds, from which the Dock authorities made their diurnal selection. That wages ruled low, was a matter to be expected, when, added to the pangs of personal hunger, the vivid picture of half-famished little ones at home, with their pleading and haunting faces ever present, spurred the gaunt applicant for work, to seek and obtain it at any cost. All honour, to the resolute and humane leaders, who organised such a seething mass of humanity, and forced a solution of the low-pay difficulty. British legislators, and industrial rulers, should learn the great social fact, that no man has fully sensed the terribly real meaning of life, unless he has had the actual dread of hunger for himself and dependent children staring him in the face. This matter of gaunt poverty should be borne in mind, as it affects this subject as no other could. Hunger, supplies the motive power to revolution. The people, in daily-increasing numbers, are getting hungry. It is not yet a question of mere bread. There are many wants in the complex social life of the present time. There are, therefore, many kinds of hunger. There is the hunger for decent housing and clothing. There is also a hunger for some rational enjoyment in life, and for moderate pensions in old age. None of these reasonable wants can be supplied to the masses unless British industries are fostered.

As a signal instance of the destruction of the interest of British workers by the indirect influence of free-imports, the case of the Bradford Strike, affords far-reaching instruction. In the Manningham Mills, thousands of workers were engaged in the manufacture of velvet and plush goods, largely for the American market Many of the hands had bought the house which they lived in, out of their earnings, while others owned shares in local Companies. Peace, and a fair measure of prosperity, appeared to reign over the district, when thunder came from a clear sky. The American Government, without, as it seemed, a day's warning, passed what was known as the McKinley Act, and the peace, progress, and prosperity of Bradford were shattered at a stroke. The Act, in connection with drastic fiscal changes, greatly increased the duty on velvet, plush, and woollen goods. The Directors of the Bradford Mills, made an attempt to retain the American trade in despite of the almost prohibitive tariff, by cutting down their profits and making a reduction of twenty-five per cent. in the wages of the operatives The latter refused (who would not?) to labour on such terms, and a great, but useless, strike ensued. Tumult and riot ran their fierce and devastating course for many weeks, while misery and suffering abounded upon every side.

The enquiry will naturally arise as to the connection between the policy of free-imports and the American tariff. How could free-imports be responsible for the McKinley Bill, or the Bradford riots? The rulers of nations, in their law-making experiments, appear to be subject to the same law as that which governs the special direction of force, viz., " the law of the least resistance." The American legislators were pressed by many of their citizens to give more substantial protection to particular industries, and fearing no practical opposition from the only nation (Great Britain) who had the greatest right to object, they followed the line of " the least resistance " and added the Ohio Senator's Bill to the large mass of protective legislation already existing. No nation, except the British, possessed much right to antagonise the measure. Other countries have one and all become protective in their respective fiscal policy. The British people alone of all the world, yield, and freely accord to the vast surplus productions of the United States, an untaxed market. A declaration on the part of Great Britain, to tax American wheat, meat, lumber, tinned fish and fruit, musical instruments, joinery, and watches, in the event of such an Act as that introduced by Mr. McKinley, coming into force, would have strangled the selfish measure at its birth, as far as England was concerned. The fearful political storm which would assuredly have risen in the

South, Middle, and Western States, at the mere whisper of a tax on the above-named articles by the British Government, would have clearly indicated the direction in which the line of "least resistance" lay. The policy of free-imports, is directly responsible for all the hostile tariffs enacted since 1878, and, indirectly, the parent of the strikes and the riots which have followed in the wake of trade depression. Hostile tariffs destroy profits on exports. Notices of reduction in wages, follow loss of profit. A threatened lowering of wages prompts, and, in many instances, necessitates a strike. The latter frequently leads to riot A sufficient number of strikes, with the accompanying demons of tumult and riot, and an industrial revolution has, like a torch-kindled forest, started on an inextinguishably devouring course. Will the peace and social security of England ever be menaced by such strife and lawlessness? Let the responsible politician take heed. The industrial decadence in each productive centre, and the consequent degradation and discontent of the labour army, are pregnant with meaning, and whispering revolt. The murmer of the last angry mutterings attending the strike of the workers in the great cotton section of Britain's textile industry, which contributes one half of the British exports, has but just subsided, by the enactment of a temporary hunger-enforcing agreement. The trial of strength between the operatives and the mill-owners, was occasioned by a prospective fall in wages of the former, which the latter justified by the existing depression in the trade. The unworkable condition of the cotton industry at modern living wages, is, in the main, traceable to the permanent policy of free-imports. British cotton fabrics are heavily taxed, and unfairly treated in every foreign port in the world. Added to this, cotton weaving machinery has been carried to India, and poor Hindoo's forced into uncivilised competition with the factory-law bound British operative. The factory laws, are humane and just, but there should be no exemptions from their operation in any portion of Britain's possessions.

Bi-Metallists ascribe the depressed and restricted condition of the cotton trade, to scarcity of money. Trade, some of them assert, was good when money was plentiful, thereby seeking to enforce the assumption that, a plethora of the medium of exchange, ensures industrial activity. The balance of evidence is on the reverse side of the contention. Profitable productive operations, produce ample means of exchange. Good trade, commands an adequate monetary circulation, while money itself is often quite powerless to stimulate commerce. The medium of exchange, is more like a servant than a master. At the present moment, scores of millions of money are lying idle in the Banks, without hope of even partial employment at the present juncture. It is the conditions which environ industry, and not the quantity of money, which determine its success or failure. Free-imports, under modern fiscal developments, inflict blow upon blow upon British industry, and the injuries are the more destructive, inasmuch, as they are of a subtle, indirect, and esoteric character.

An examination of another branch of the question will not be profitless. Of Britain's mineral resources—the magically golden keys which have unlocked the doors of England's industrial wealth—coal has an easy prominence. Yet, of this commodity, Britain has been lavish to an extraordinary degree of prodigality. Thirty millions of tons of the finest quality has been freely exported annually, for years past, and principally to the industrial competitors of England.* Despite this large export, and to a considerable extent, as a consequence of it, Great Britain has been unable to employ all her coal miners—six-hundred-and-fifty thousand in number—at a living wage. Notice of a twenty-five per cent. reduction, on the forty per cent. advance in wages during the prosperous years,

---

* *The Times*, of September 20th, 1893, writing on the proposed Coal Trust Scheme, remarks :—"Next after water and bread, coal is recognized to be the most general necessity of English life. To waste it is to waste the tissues of our strength ; to economise the production and to prolong the duration of the supply is proportionately to prolong the period during which we may hope to hold a first place among the nations. It is no exaggeration, therefore, to say that there can hardly be a proposal of greater importance to consider, than one which would materially affect our manner of dealing with these vast possessions." Such language on the part of *The Times* is tantamount to a strong condemnation of the wholesale exportation of coal, which late years have witnessed. Exports, which the great decline in British industry rendered possible. Would not a national coal trust, finding the domestic demand for fuel, on account of bad trade, insufficient to make a dividend, ship vast quantities to half the world and denude the country of its precious mineral ? Is not an export tax on coal a necessity for national industrial safety ?

has recently been given. The reason assigned for the cutting-down of labour's share in the outcome of the pits, is, the general and widespread stagnation in trade. Why should the miners consent to share all the burdens of a glut in the market, and a fall in prices, traceable, from a retrospective industrial and fiscal analysis of the subject, to the policy of free-imports? Vast stocks of coal exist, partly in consequence of one hundred thousand workers, from partially collapsed industries, drifting into the mining districts, thus raising the total number of mining efficients, to that extent, in excess of the normal demand ; and in part from the great shrinkage in the requirements of the coal-consuming trades. But should the workers dumbly suffer all the loss and the misery of the resultant re-actions of so senseless a system as free-imports? The miners practically say no, by initiating a national strike.

These re-current miners' strikes are ominous. There is a progressive peril, developing with each successive refusal to labour on semi-starvation terms. The displaced workers from many crippled industries, seek for labour at the active pit, and thus the poor colliers receive a double hurt First the loss of the demand for coal from the failing industries, and the competition also of the workless operatives. From both causes combined, they are unable to resist long the pressure for a fall in wages. But Statesmen should take heed. The coal mining industry is the largest organised concreted productive enterprise in the country. As it is the largest, in the massed workers sense, it is also the most dangerous and difficult to deal with.

What a national gain it would be, if a hundred thousand miners could find profitable employment on the land, from which vast numbers originally came. If the iron, steel, wool, and hardware trades could absorb another hundred thousand, what a beneficial change in the collier's prospects would be effected. Such extremely desirable re-distribution of workers is an idle dream, while the system of free-imports prevail. Yet, even in the present time of industrial peril, there are politicians of the front rank who will tell working men, as if to comfort them in their trade distress, that they have the inestimable blessing of free-trade, or their trouble would be immeasurably greater. It is an untruth, a shame-faced and a cruelly deceptive falsehood. The day is approaching at an event-devouring pace, when such blind leaders will have to reckon with a tardily-enlightened and politically abused people. Free-trade does not exist. For the thousandth time, it is necessary to shatter the idol, and proclaim the truth. Free-imports are not free-trade.

When the recorded opinions on the subject of such public men as Lord Playfair, Sir John Lubbuck, Sir Thomas Farrer, and Mr Leonard Courtney, are calmly examined, the marvel is, that reasoners of their calibre should fail to perceive the noon-day truth of Britain's gigantic fiscal error.* Success would cover many defects. But the industry-crumbling failure of free-imports demand, and necessitate, immediate reform. The masses cannot be expected to trace cause and effect, and solve problems of economic and fiscal importance. But they hold in strict account those public leaders whose duty it is to safely steer the national industrial bark.

The people lose their employment, and find themselves starving in the streets. The only assimilated fact, in connection with their deplorable condition, is, the closing of the works in which their weekly wages were earned. They meet in crowds and clamour for work. The mill-owners, finding that the price at which each successive foreign tariff compels them to dispose of their commodities, leaves them no margin of profit, and, in not infrequent instances, inflicts a loss; they reluctantly, and from grim necessity, close their works. One centre of

---

* The Delegates from the Associated Chambers of Commerce, have held their annual meeting. But what have they decided to recommend as a remedy for the degraded condition of British industry? None, that is in any appreciable degree adequate. The year 1893, like preceding years, finds the great majority of the members hopelessly befogged on the question of a practical solution of the difficulty. A few enlightened minds make their voices heard, amid the confusion of small talk, and manfully endeavour to carry a vote for drastic fiscal reform. All honour to their patriotic courage and zeal. If the members of the commercial Parliament were, one and all, fairly chosen representatives of *Chambers of Industry*, the much needed reform for placing British production on a sound and profitable basis, would not long be delayed. The trade with Siam, concerning which the Chambers forced a resolution into prominence, is a small matter compared with the hostile tariffs of the whole

bread-winning activity after the other, stay the tread of busy feet, and still the throbbing pulse of many shafts and spindles, and the towns, with their innumerable stores, gradually reflect the people's industrial sorrow, and the foreign investors—who sustain free-imports—ride through the streets and, on seeing the desolation, mutter something of economic law, and the necessity of putting their money in the cheapest producing centres. Meanwhile, the people wait and hope for the return of the tide of industrial prosperity, which gladdened their hearts in the by-gone years. But without reform—the return of such prosperity is hopeless. And in the coming days a feverishness and restlessness may come upon the trade-mocked workers. Some of the strongest from the various districts may migrate to distant places in search of work : to glean the sad experience only of discovering the inhabitants equally unemployed, and similarly depressed.

---

world, against which British exports have to contend. But the Chambers shut their eyes to these facts.

Sir Albert Rollit, M.P., in his presidential address, after the assurance that trade was slowly improving, warned his hearers against what he called, the pseudo-economical expedients and hindrances, of fair-trade and retaliation What of the perils and danger to British production, from free-imports of competing goods and the war of tariffs? On this subject, not a suggestion was offered. If any improvement in British industry takes place, it will come out of the bone and sinew of the workers, by a general reduction in wages. Who can deny the assertion? Not the somewhat adroit master of assumptions, the President of the Associated Chambers of Commerce.

The British people will have to instruct the Chambers, for it is as clear as noon-day, that the Chambers are unable to teach and lead the people.

Murmurings in particular would speedily become general. The units would swell to tens. The tens to hundreds. The hundreds to thousands. Village would join with village, and town with town. A vast, unmanageable, and overshadowing army of unemployed would come into existence. An army, discontented, hungry, hopeless, and politically guideless. Numerous detached masses of weary and despondent workers drifting into crude association, would shake the power of the country. All the conditions of possible revolution would be in full development. To day, the various groups might be dealt with separately. To-morrow, by some electrical free-masonry, the whole army of unemployed may be organized, and making demands upon the Government impossible of fulfilment. There would be marches and counter-marches; parleying held, and mass resolutions passed. Hopelessness and despair would degrade their manhood, and partially dethrone their reason. The idle, the dissolute. and the lawless from the dregs of town life, would hang upon the rear of every column, and surround the border of each crowd, jealously watching for opportunities to plunder, and openings for crime. Society would be powerless, because it would have ceased, in a great measure, to exist. Reform, too long delayed, could not, by its promise, bring immediate relieving power. Open and undisguised industrial revolution, with its violent self-righting and destructive tendencies, would bar the way. May such calamity be averted.

Timely reform, or politico-industrial revolution. Which?

SHALL BRITISH INDUSTRIES PERISH?

PROPOSED

ACT OF PARLIAMENT

TO ENFORCE

FREE-TRADE FOR BRITISH EXPORTS,

BY MEANS OF

RETALIATION,

AND TO SECURE

A FREE HOME MARKET FOR ENGLISH GOODS

BY AN EQUALISING

TAX ON COMPETING FOREIGN PRODUCTS.

This Act is entitled: An Act to amend the policy of Free-Imports (inaccurately named Free-Trade), and to secure Free-Trade for British Productions, at home and abroad.

PREAMBLE.

WHEREAS

> The policy of free-imports—sanctioned by the British people as an experimental example to other nations—has encouraged, if not actually promoted the hostile tariffs which render the export of British goods unprofitable and frequently impossible, and permits unfair foreign competition in the home market, is an unjust system of international trading most injurious to the producing masses of the country :

AND WHEREAS

> A policy of free-trade—*i.e.*, a system of free-exchange, free-selling in addition to free-buying—would remove restrictions from commerce, the policy of free-imports is responsible for the barriers which have been raised against British exports, causing enormous losses to English trade, and many thousands of British workers to lose their employment :

AND WHEREAS

The principle of free-trade ensures a total absence of duties on all sides alike, or an equality of taxation on foreign and home productions, rendering commerce free to every competitor by giving the same economic conditions to each, the policy of free-imports *taxes the British producer only*, while a free market is unjustly offered to Great Britain's industrial rivals :

AND WHEREAS

It is necessary, in the interest of the masses, that such daily necessaries as tea, coffee, cocoa, raisins, and currants, which cannot be produced in the British Isles, *should be admitted duty free* :

AND WHEREAS

It is of paramount importance in regard to the stability of the British Empire, that a distinct preference be given to the commodities imported from any portion of the British Dominions :

AND WHEREAS

It is for the national welfare that the British production of food and manufactured commodities should be increased to the utmost extent, that the masses may be fully employed at good rates of pay :

AND WHEREAS

The policy of free-imports restricts the home growth of food, and its profitable exchange, and also the internal and external trade in British goods, it is expedient, and vitally important, to pass an Act regulating the international commerce of Great Britain, in order to secure just and sound economic conditions for British products in the home market, and to enforce an approximation of free-trade for English and Irish exports, in the markets of the world.

BE IT, THEREFORE, ENACTED :—

THE BILL.

CLAUSE I.

EQUAL CONDITIONS FOR ALL.

1. THAT

   After the passing of this Act, every article of a competing nature entering British ports shall pay an equalising duty, equivalent to the amount of local and Imperial taxation borne by the British producer of the same class of goods.

2. THAT

   An International Trading Commission shall be appointed under this Act, whose duty it shall be to classify and to schedule all articles imported, and to decide which goods are of a competing kind and which are not, and to fix the amount of the equalising duty to be paid on the competing classes of imports.

A FREE BREAKFAST-TABLE.

3. *THAT*

Tea, coffee, cocoa, currants, and raisins (non-competing articles) shall be admitted duty free.

CLAUSE II.

A COMPULSARY CLAUSE FOR FREE-TRADE.

1. *THAT*

The competing imports of goods from any country which imposes an import duty on British and Irish competing exports, which exceeds—taking ad valorem and specific duties combined—the average amount of 15 per cent., shall be subjected to a retaliatory duty, equal in amount to the duty placed upon British goods entering such country.

2. *THAT*

The weapon of a retaliatory duty shall be used in a strictly international defensive sense, and discarded at the earliest date after it has served its specific purpose.

3. *THAT*

Retaliatory duties shall not be imposed for the purpose of protecting any particular British industry, but simply as a means to break down unjust fiscal barriers.

CLAUSE III.

PREFERENTIAL TRADING WITH THE COLONIES

THAT

All competing imports from the British Colonies and Possessions shall be admitted at a reduction of 50 per cent. off the amount of the equalising duty imposed on the goods of foreign nations, provided, that the Colonies and British Possessions, make a substantial reduction of their tariffs in favour of British exports.

INDEX.

INDEX.

	PAGE
Agriculture—fall in price of products	89
America, free-trade by—a bad thing for England	21
Argentina, British investment in	61
Banking, Clearing House Returns of	37
Bi-Metalists, contention of, in relation to bad times	132
Bradford, industries of—influence of the McKinley Tariff	129
Bread, nominally cheap, but what is its real price?	69
Britain (Great) Rip Van Winkle dream of	29
British Empire, moral power of	86
Capitalists, investment, choice of	31
Chartists—result of free-imports foreseen	85
Cheapness, relative nature of	115
Cleveland (President) free-trade, views of	90
Coal, export of, during the period of free-imports	49
Coal, importance of	133
Colonies, preference for by France, Germany, and Spain	82
Colliers, number of	50
Commerce, Associated Chambers of	136
Cotton (cloth) weaving of by Hindoos	17
Cotton (raw) consumption of in India	18
Cotton (raw)—export tax to be placed on by the Americans	28
Crow (Sir Joseph)—Report on English and French trade since 1881	82
Duties, abolition, date of	45

	PAGE
Eight Hours—the relation of wages thereto	105
England—declining trade thereof	8
England, the future markets of	13
Exchange, equation of	41
Exports—their nature and falling off	59
Exports, value of, in prosperous years	11
Farmers (British)—their share of free-trade demanded	26
Federation, Commercial Inter-British	80
Food, imports of	117
France, silks imported from	51
France, Cobden treaty with	63
Free Breakfast-Table	145
Free-Imports—not sanctioned by the British people	21
Free-Imports—price of bread since its adoption	26
Free-Imports—protection in other countries rendered profitable thereby	57
Free-Imports—reasons for opposing same	13
Free-Imports, policy of, sanctioned as an experiment	141
Free-Imports—points to be remembered	97
Free-Imports, policy of—questions regarding its failure	13
Free-Trade, non-existence of	15
Free-Trade—argument for its one-sided application refuted	16
Free-Trade—the title as a correct description of Britain's fiscal policy, denied	75
Free-Trade—its non-success as a policy of free-imports	77
Gold, appreciation of	114
Government (Party)—inflexible and machine-like	125

	PAGE
Hindoos, daily labour, price of	88
Hindoos—rivals of British workmen	19
Imports—fully manufactured goods, amount of	53
Labour, hours of, the condition of British industry when the ten and the nine hours reform was passed	108
Labour, protection of, but freedom for the product	39
Labour, wages of, since fourteenth century	121
Liberals, party cry of	98
Loaf (four pound) price of in 1812	113
Manchester, appeal to	29
Manufacture (foreign) forty years ago	100
Mill (J. Stuart)—hostile tariffs, how to prevent loss therefrom	56
Miners, strikes of	134
Newspapers, no competition from American and German editions	103
Paupers, cost of	62
Population—exports and imports in relation thereto	65
Press, writers of, and free-imports	89
Product—same product, same tax	40
Producer, defence of	91
Profits, tariffs, an operation on the margin of	32
Prosperity, British industrial, cause of	67
Protection, commencement of, in Europe	55
Protection, in the old sense, impossible	27
Protection, profitable nature of	55
Protection—part played in prosperity of other nations	68
Retaliation, need of	24
Revolution, politico-industrial	138

	PAGE
Shipping, tonnage of	62
Statesmen, attitude of	123
Strikes (great) names of	127
Tariffs (foreign), increase of, since 1846	92
Tariffs (British) in their incidence press more heavily on the poor than the rich	78
Tariffs—who pays them on competing imports	34
Taxation, Imperial and local, burden of	110
United States, British retaliation, effect of	130
Wages—free-imports in relation thereto	94
Wages—meaning of reduction	8
Wealth (national)—France, America, and England contrasted	74
Wheat, price of, since fourteenth century	121
Wheat, national stock of	83

APPENDIX.

APPENDIX.

To those readers who may experience a difficulty in rightly apprehending the true position of the writer—a self-styled, real free-trader, proposing the imposition of tariffs, and a professed opponent of Protection, insisting upon the fiscal defence of British industry—the following brief explanation may be of service.

Free-Trade, if it existed, would remove restrictions from imports and exports, and institute a system of free exchange. The policy of free-imports, has failed to enlarge the freedom of British trade and industries. On the contrary, it has indirectly caused an increase in the restrictions to British trade, by the encouragement of foreign tariffs. British exports are hindered and restricted to a far greater extent under the policy of free-imports—inaccurately named free-trade—than they ever were in the old protectionist days. Of what use is it for a nation to buy freely, if it is unable to sell unrestrictedly? Even in the home market the British people dispose of their products under burdens and hindrances, from which the foreigner is free. The latter has a free entry to British markets, and contributes nothing to the support of the English Government. The British food-raiser, and other producers, are compelled to bear the whole net-work of taxation. Is this free-trade? Foreign nations possess a larger measure of free-trade than the British people. They have their own market, to which any neighbouring nation has entrance only by paying the full share of the market toll, and the

British free-market also. Where is the free-market for British exports ? Not one exists, not even at home. The fiscal condition which would render the home market a free one to the British people themselves, has not been fulfilled. The foreigner has not been mulcted in the same taxation for the use of the British market, as the home producer is compelled to bear. Hence, no equality of taxation—the essential feature of free-trade—exists. Therefore, no free-trade exists, even at home. The nation which obtains the largest measure of free-exchange, enjoys the greatest amount of free-trade. Of what earthly use is it for the British people to shout free-trade, when none exists for them. There is, however, a pitiable side to it. The masses have not had their eyes fully opened to the delusion, and they starve in their thousands for the want of work, when ample employment might soon be forthcoming. Great Britain who is supposed to enjoy the blessing of free-trade, is, in reality, the greatest protectionist country in the world. But it is in giving protection to the goods of the foreigner, and not to the products of her own people, in which the protectionist tendency exists.

No supporter of England's present policy of free-imports, has the smallest right to call himself a free-trader. He is, in practice, far more of a protectionist than a free-trader. Once, this true aspect of the case enters his mind, he will strive to obtain a measure of real free-trade, by helping to enforce it. No good thing in this life comes by the mere asking for it. It has to be earned. The writer has submitted a true and consistent argument all through the preceding pages, and has left no fact of real importance out of the calculation. He is a thoroughly consistent free-trader, and one who firmly believes that protection, *per se*, for nations, is a thing of the past. The mechanical science of the world is too far advanced, and much too diffused for nations to need it. To Empires like the British, approximate free-trade within, is a *sine qua non* for its existence. Universal free-trade must be relegated to the distant future, so long as the British policy of free-imports prevail. To those who fear a return to protection, it is well for them to remember, that a nation can but have a million and a half of workers idle, a million of paupers, seven millions of acres of land out of cultivation, and thousands of mills and factories closed, or working short time. To say nothing of the national strikes. Can things be worse? In looking forward to evils from a return to protection, why pass over the ills from which we are suffering under the system of free-imports. Those that urge that they are as bad off in other countries, condemn themselves. If protectionist nations suffer no worse under their tariffs, than England does under what is fondly called free-trade, where is the boasted superiority of the British practice? It is not true, however, that foreign nations are doing as badly, relatively, as Great Britain. It is a shamed-faced assertion, constantly reiterated in the press, without adequate proofs in its support.*

Then there are those who fear that a duty on wheat or food would simply raise prices for the benefit of the

---

* For detailed information concerning the relatively greater progress made by foreign nations, the reader is referred to the British Jugernath, an able work by Sir Guildford Molesworth.

landlords, who would increase their rents. There is small ground for this dread. The agricultural labourers and the tenant farmers will demand any increase in prices as their rightful share. The landlords would do sufficiently well by getting their rents, which they are unable to do at the present time.

Free-Traders must reach down their dictionary, and turn to the definition of free-trade.

The writer, in his somewhat extended experience at public meetings among working men, has never failed to convince them of the soundness of his position, and of his right to the title of free-trader.

An attempt, on the part of Great Britain, to enforce a large measure of free-trade upon her industrial rivals, would not be equivalent to an insistence of a system of international trading which had failed in her own case. Free-Trade has not *failed*, because it has never *existed*.

www.ingramcontent.com/pod-product-compliance
Lightning Source LLC
Chambersburg PA
CBHW030308170426
43202CB00009B/918